Ribbon
Artistry

20 Original Projects by Noted Designers

CREATIVE
PUBLISHING
international

Copyright © 2002
Creative Publishing international, Inc.
5900 Green Oak Drive
Minnetonka, Minnesota 55343
1-800-328-3895
www.creativepub.com
All rights reserved
Printed in U.S.A.

President/CEO: Michael Eleftheriou
Vice President/Publisher: Linda Ball

RIBBON ARTISTRY
Created by: The Editors of Creative Publishing international

Executive Editor: Elaine Perry
Managing Editor: Yen Le
Senior Editor: Linda Neubauer
Art Directors: Stephanie Michaud, Deborah Pierce
Project & Prop Stylist: Joanne Wawra
Samplemakers: Arlene Dohrman, Sheila Duffy
Photo Stylists: Arlene Dohrman, Christine Jahns, Joanne Wawra
Studio Services Manager: Marcia Chambers
Photographers: Chuck Nields, Andrea Rugg
Director of Production Services: Kim Gerber
Contributors: Bucilla; C.M. Offray & Son, Inc.; DMC Corporation;
June Tailor, Inc.; Mokuba Ribbons; YLI Corporation

ISBN 1-58923-019-1

Printed on American paper by:
Quebecor World
10 9 8 7 6 5 4 3 2 1

Library of Congress Cataloging-in-Publication Data

Ribbon artistry.
    p. cm.
    ISBN 1-58923-019-1 (pbk.)
    1. Ribbon work.   I. Creative Publishing International.
TT850.5 .R5 2001
746'.0476--dc21

                    2001047037

Creative Publishing international, Inc. offers a variety of how-to books.
For information write:
    Creative Publishing international, Inc.
     Subscriber Books
    5900 Green Oak Drive
    Minnetonka, MN 55343

Acknowledgements

Special thanks to the
following ribbon artists:
Janna Britton

Janis Bullis

Phyllis Dobbs

Beverly Hofmann

Markena Lanska

Sandra McCooey

Nancy Overton

Carole Rodgers

Contents

Miles & Miles of Ribbon

Whether embellishing home furnishings or detailing garments and fashion accessories, ribbons add lively colors and touchable textures. Our long-standing fascination with ribbons has generated a variety of creative ribbon manipulation techniques, giving avid crafters many ways to use these versatile, supple strands to beautify the world. Many of these techniques are taught on pages 10 to 33. Given these basic methods and some creative exploration, the ribbon artistry possibilities are endless.

The projects in this book are originals, designed by experienced ribbon artists whose explorations have taken them in various creative directions. Each artist was given a few simple guidelines and the free reign to design ribbon-crafting projects with the techniques, ribbon colors, and styles that reflected her own taste and touch. The resulting mix of projects includes items sure to tantalize every ribbon enthusiast, whether your interest lies in ribbon embroidery, making ribbon flowers, or creating intriguing ribbon trims. Rather than provide specific brand names and numbers for the project ribbons, generic descriptions are provided as suggestions. We encourage you to explore the miles and miles of ribbons available to you and to select ribbons for your projects that work for your decor, your mood, or your fashion taste.

Ribbon Styles

The projects are designed for woven-edge ribbons: narrow strips of fabric with tiny selvages finishing the outer edges. These ribbons are available in an amazing range of styles, textures, and colors, with choices suitable for every occasion and every decorating scheme. Woven-edge ribbons come in a dozen standard widths, ranging from ⅟₁₆" to 3½" (1.5 to 89 mm); occasionally you will find ribbons woven to a nonstandard width. Silk ribbons for embroidery come in assorted sizes designed for that craft.

Woven-edge ribbons are generally washable and colorfast, though this information may not be included on the label. It is a good idea to test-wash a sample before using it in a garment or home decor item. For items that will be laundered, both the fabric and the ribbon should be preshrunk by laundering.

Silks

Taffetas

Satins. Woven to produce a glossy, smooth surface on one side (single-face) or both sides (double-face), satin ribbons are suitable for many applications and manipulation techniques. They come in a rainbow of solid colors with plain or feather-edge finishes.

Narrow silks. Silk and silk substitute ribbons, discussed in more detail on page 30, are designed specifically for embroidery. They are very drapable and, though delicate looking, sturdy enough to be pulled repeatedly through fabric without suffering damage.

Taffetas. Taffeta ribbons have a fine, plain weave that makes them reversible with smooth, slightly lustrous surfaces. Often they have fine copper wires woven into the selvages for extra body and to allow them to be shaped. Taffeta ribbons include ombré and variegated styles (1) that shade from dark to light or from one color to another across the ribbon width. There are also taffetas with woven plaids and checks (2). Shot-effect taffetas (3) are woven with contrasting colors in the warp and weft that create an iridescent look. Moiré taffetas (4) have a water-mark design embossed onto the surface.

Grosgrains. The weave
structure of grosgrain ribbons creates
a matte appearance with
a distinctive crosswise rib. These
sturdy ribbons are available in solid
colors as well as striped,
dotted, and patterned styles.

Jacquards. These ribbons
feature woven-in designs,
either single color or multicolor,
resembling miniature tapestries.
Metallic threads may be
incorporated into the designs,
which include florals,
geometrics, and other figures.

*Grosgrains
and Jacquards*

Sheers

Sheers. Finely woven, transparent ribbons in a range of widths are used to create gossamer, feminine effects. Many have monofilament woven into the selvages for support; wire-edge sheer ribbons are also available. Sheer ribbons often have satin or metallic stripes.

Velvets. Like velvet fabric, these ribbons have a cut pile that is soft and luxurious to the touch and gives extra depth to their colors.

≈ Weaving ≈

Ribbons, in an array of colors, sizes, and textures, are woven together to create exquisite fabric. Given a few basic weave patterns, a vast choice of ribbons, and an eagerness to experiment, the design possibilities for woven ribbon fabric are endless. Woven ribbon may accent parts of garments, such as pockets, lapels, yokes, cuffs, or vest fronts. Personal items like small handbags, sachets, book covers, or glasses cases can be made entirely from woven ribbon fabric. In home decor, woven ribbon can be featured on pillows, fancy chair seats, placemats and table runners, or picture frames.

A padded, gridded pinning board is extremely handy for this technique. A well-padded ironing board also can be used, if it is large enough to accommodate the entire project. It is a good idea to make test samples of a few weave patterns, using different ribbon color and size arrangements, to help you determine the most desirable look for your project. The chart opposite will help you determine the total amount of ribbon necessary for your project. For two-way weaves, divide the number of ribbons used into the total to estimate the length of each ribbon needed. As with other woven fabrics, the lengthwise ribbons are referred to as the warp and the crosswise ribbons are the weft.

Materials:

- *Ribbons*
- *Tracing paper*
- *Lightweight fusible knit interfacing*
- *Padded, gridded pinning board*
- *Glass-head pins*
- *Bodkin, elastic guides, or large-eyed blunt needle*
- *Scissors*
- *Iron and pressing cloth*

Basic Weaving

1 Trace the pattern seamline and cutting line onto tracing paper; mark the desired grainline for the warp ribbons. Pin the pattern face-up on the pinning board, aligning the grainline to the grid. Cut interfacing larger than the pattern, and place it, fusible side up, over the pattern. Pin.

2 Cut ribbons for the warp (vertical rows), 2" (5 cm) longer than the pattern; place them side by side on the padded surface over the interfacing, aligning them to the grainline. Pin each ribbon at top and bottom, angling pins away from the pattern.

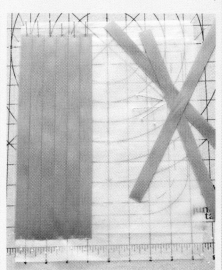

3 Thread weft ribbons onto bodkin, elastic guide, or large-eyed needle. Weave weft ribbons through warp ribbons, following the desired weave pattern. Begin at the top and work down, pulling every row taut and straight and abutting edges as closely as possible. Cut and pin each ribbon in turn.

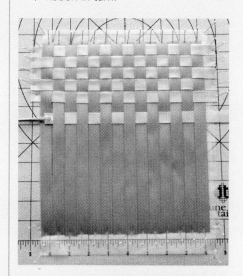

4 Cover woven piece with press cloth; press lightly to partially fuse interfacing to piece. Remove pins. Place piece face-down; press again to completely fuse interfacing. Cut and sew piece into project as desired.

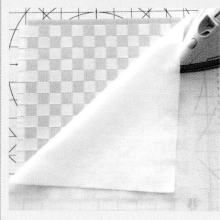

Ribbon Width	Total Length Needed		
2-way weaves	4" (10 cm) square	8" (20.5 cm) square	12" (30.5 cm) square
³/₁₆" (5 mm)	6½ yd. (5.95 m)	22 yd. (20.3 m)	46 yd. (42.5 m)
¼" (7 mm)	4½ yd. (4.15 m)	16 yd. (14.7 m)	33 yd. (30.4 m)
³/₈" (9 mm)	3¾ yd. (3.45 m)	12 yd. (11 m)	25 yd. (23 m)
½" (12 mm)	3¼ yd. (3 m)	9¾ yd. (8.95 m)	20¼ yd. (18.7 m)
⅝" (15 mm)	2½ yd. (2.3 m)	7¼ yd. (6.65 m)	15¼ yd. (14 m)
⅞" (23 mm)	1½ yd. (1.4 m)	5 yd. (4.6 m)	10 yd. (9.15 m)

Ribbon Width	Length for Each Ribbon		
Tumbling blocks	4" (10 cm) square	8" (20.5 cm) square	12" (30.5 cm) square
³/₁₆" (5 mm)	3½ yd. (3.2 m)	12 yd. (11 m)	25 yd. (23 m)
¼" (7 mm)	2½ yd. (2.3 m)	9 yd. (8.25 m)	18½ yd. (17 m)
³/₈" (9 mm)	2¼ yd. (2.1 m)	7 yd. (6.4 m)	14½ yd. (13.4 m)
½" (12 mm)	2 yd. (1.85 m)	5½ yd. (5.05 m)	12 yd. (11.04 m)
⅝" (15 mm)	1½ yd. (1.4 m)	4¼ yd. (3.9 m)	10 yd. (9.15 m)
⅞" (23 mm)	1 yd. (.92 m)	3½ yd. (3.2 m)	7 yd. (6.4 m)

Weave Patterns

Plain weave: Pass weft over one warp, under one, over one, under one, continuing across. Reverse the pattern with each succeeding row.

Basket weave: Pass weft over two warp, under two, over two, under two, continuing across. Repeat the pattern for the next row. Reverse the pattern for the next two rows.

Twill weave: Pass weft over two warp, under one, over two, under one, continuing across. In second row and each succeeding row, shift the pattern one warp ribbon to the right, creating a diagonal pattern. If woven in alternating light and dark colors in both warp and weft, a diagonal zigzag is created.

Tumbling blocks: Weave two diagonal sets of ribbons, in two different colors, at a 30° angle through warp ribbons of a third color. Weave the first diagonal set from upper left to lower right, passing over one, under two, continuing across. Shift the pattern one ribbon with each row. Weave the second set from lower left to upper right, passing over two warps, under one, passing under the first set of diagonals, continuing across. Shift the pattern one ribbon with each row.

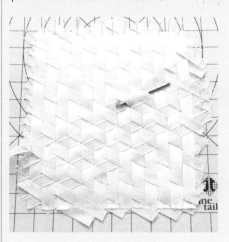

Braiding

Braided ribbon trims have interesting textural patterns that vary, depending on the ribbons used, from subtle, tailored, or dainty to bold, elegant, or flamboyant. Because they are quite flexible, they can be shaped in gentle curves when necessary. Simple three-ply braids can become the spaghetti straps for a chic dress. A multicolored four-ply satin ribbon sash may be braided for a little girl's party dress. Petite satin ribbon loop braid offers a charming finish for the hem of an infant's christening gown or the edging around a bride's slippers. Braids of various styles and sizes are perfect for hat brims, headbands, or barrettes or for home decor items like napkin rings, lampshade edgings, tieback accents, or bell pulls.

A padded pinning surface is useful for most braiding techniques, as ribbon ends can be secured, leaving both hands free to braid. Most ribbons up to 7/8" (23 mm) wide can be braided successfully; however, flat multiple-ply braiding is more successful with narrower ribbons, especially grosgrains. Rolled braiding and loop braiding expose both sides of the ribbon, which can create interesting looks with single-face satins. Finish the ends of braided trims by turning raw edges to the back and hand-tacking. Stitch ends together and hide raw edges on the underside to form a circle.

Materials:
- *Ribbons*
- *Padded pinning surface*
- *Glass-head pins*
- *Needle and thread*

Flat Three-ply Braiding

Cut three ribbons about one-sixth longer than desired finished length of trim. Pin ribbons side by side on a padded pinning surface. Pass the left ply over the middle, then right over middle, continuing in this pattern; always keep the ribbons facing up and relatively flat.

Rolled Three-ply Braiding

Cut three ribbons about one-sixth longer than desired finished length of trim. Pin ribbons side by side on a padded pinning surface. Roll the left ply over the middle, then right over middle, continuing in this pattern. Keep even tension on all three ribbons; the outer edges will form straight lines.

Rolled Four-ply Braiding

1 Cut four ribbons about one-third longer than desired finished length of trim. Pin ribbons in sets of two at right angles to each other; weave them together as shown. Roll the two left ribbons to the right at right angles.

2 Roll the far right ribbon under the adjacent ribbon, over the next, and under the last. Repeat with the ribbon that is now on the far right.

3 Roll the two left ribbons to the right at right angles. Repeat step 2. Continue in this pattern to the desired length.

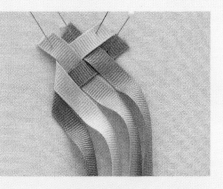

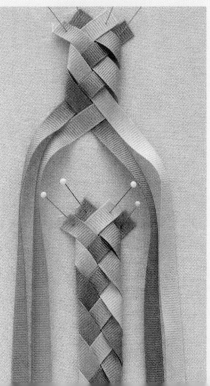

Five-ply Braiding

Cut five ribbons about one-sixth longer than desired finished length of trim. Pin ribbons side by side on a padded pinning surface. Weave the outer right ribbon over and under the other ribbons until it becomes the outer left ribbon. Repeat with ribbon that has shifted to the outer right. Continue this pattern to the desired length.

Single Ribbon Loop Braiding

Cut a length of ribbon nine times longer than the desired finished length of the trim. Form a flat loop in the center of the ribbon; hold it with your left hand. Form a twisted loop to the right of the first one; slip it over the right-hand loop and draw the loops together snugly, down to the ribbon width.

Form a flat loop in your right hand and slip it through the left loop. Draw the left loop snug. Form a flat loop in your left hand and slip it through the right loop. Draw the right loop snug. Continue in this pattern to the desired finished length.

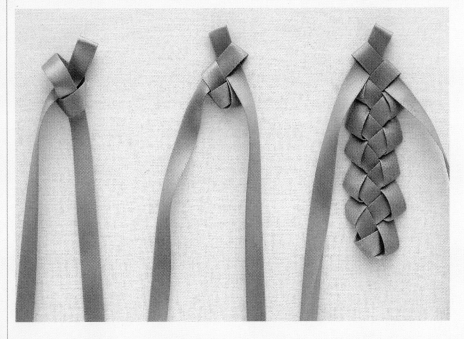

Double Ribbon Loop Braiding

Cut two ribbons, each four to five times longer than the desired finished length of the trim. Hand-tack a loop in the end of each ribbon, with an opening equal to the ribbon width. Holding one ribbon in each hand, slip the left loop through the right loop. Then braid the ribbons following the directions for single ribbon loop braiding.

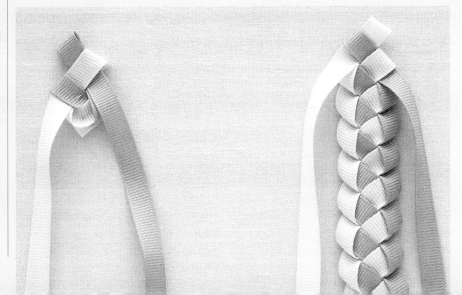

Pleating

Intriguing trims for a multitude of uses can be made simply by pleating ribbons. Often one edge of the pleated trim is stitched in place and the pleats along the free edge fan out slightly to lead the eye along the trimmed edge. In some applications, the trim may be stitched down the center, allowing both free edges to fan out. Because pleated trims are fairly flexible, they can be used around curves. Closely spaced pleats or stacked pleats offer the most flexibility.

Knife pleats and box pleats are the bases for more detailed trims that involve repetitive folding, rolling, and hand tacking. Ribbons of all sizes and types can be used, keeping in mind that the detailed trims may reveal both sides of the ribbon. If using wired ribbon for edge-stitched trims, the wire may be removed along the edge that is stitched to reduce bulk. To make directions universal for any width of ribbon, measurements are given in ribbon widths (RWs). The chart below will help you determine the total amount of ribbon necessary for trims that have evenly spaced and stacked knife and box pleats. For other styles, short test samples are the best way to estimate length.

Materials:
- *Ribbon*
- *Air-soluble marking pen*
- *Scissors*
- *Hand needle and thread*
- *Sewing machine, optional for some styles*

Pleating Style	Ribbon Length Needed
Single knife or box pleats	3 times finished length
Double knife or box pleats	5 times finished length
Triple knife or box pleats	7 times finished length

Knife Pleats

1 Mark off RWs on one selvage of the ribbon, using an air-soluble marking pen. Fold in a single, double, or triple knife pleat. Hand-stitch along one edge or down the center.

2 Fold the next pleat or set one RW from the last fold. Continue this pattern to the desired length. Turn under and stitch the end, if it will not be hidden in a seam.

If machine stitching, fold pleats toward you, stop stitching with the needle down one or two stitches into the pleat, and fold the next pleat or set. Stitch continuously.

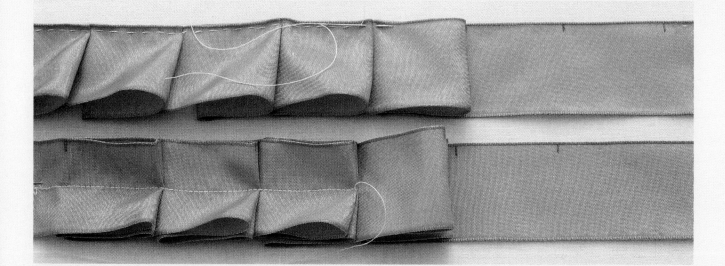

Box Pleats

1 Mark off RWs on one selvage of the ribbon, using an air-soluble marking pen. For a single box pleat, fold a stack of two pleats, ½ RW wide, folding the ribbon tail back over the stack. For a double box pleat, fold a stack of four pleats, ½ RW wide, folding the ribbon tail back over the stack. Hand-tack along one edge or at the center of the folds, taking a tiny stitch into each of the folds.

2 Open the folds into a box pleat. Hand-tack the outer edges of the folds in place at the edge or center.

3 Fold consecutive box pleats so that the folds touch. Or skip a ½ RW between folds. Stitch continuously.

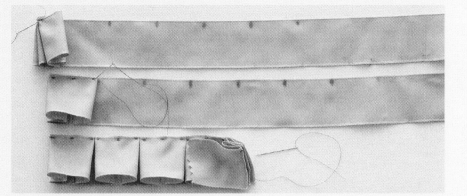

Create different looks by varying the size and spacing of the pleats and the position at which they are stitched.

1. Double 1-RW knife pleats, ½ RW between.

2. Single 1-RW knife pleats, overlapping ½ RW.

3. Clustered 1-RW knife pleats, clusters separated by 1 RW.

4. Double box pleats made with 1-RW and ½-RW folds.

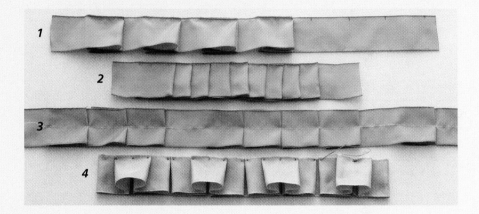

Flying Geese

Make center-tacked ½-RW knife pleat. Fold the outer corners to the center, forming a triangle; tack in place. Repeat so the point of each triangle touches the base of the adjacent one.

Pulled Box Pleats

Make center-stitched single or double box pleats, 1 RW wide. Pull the top selvages together at the center of each pleat and hand-tack.

Bow Ties

Make single box pleats 2 RWs wide. Overlap the top selvages at the center of each pleat and secure with a bead, button, or miniature ribbon flower.

❧ Gathering & Smocking ❧

Softly ruffled and bubbled ribbon trims are made with patterns of running stitches. Some of the gathering stitches can be sewn by machine, especially for wider ribbons. Hand stitching is often more secure and makes this a portable pastime. Consistent stitch length and spacing is important; multiples and fractions of ribbon widths are used for spacing. Longer stitches result in tighter, deeper gathers; shorter stitches in looser, shallower gathers. Wired ribbon can be gathered simply by pulling the wire along one edge, though for tighter gathers, the wire should be removed and the edge sewn with ¼" (6 mm) running stitches.

Smocking pulls the ribbon into soft ripples in a repeated design. It is done by pulling together and knotting groups of strategically placed stitches. The stitches are hidden on the back side of the ribbon, so only the pulled design shows on the front. Shell smocking is suitable for narrower ribbons, up to 1½" (39 mm) wide; lattice smocking is most effective on wider ribbons where at least two rows of smocking can be worked.

For both manipulation methods, soft, supple ribbons are the most successful. Some of these techniques are the bases for making ribbon flowers. Because the amount of ribbon taken up varies with the length of the running stitches and the tightness to which the gathers are pulled, work from the ribbon reel whenever possible or measure test samples to estimate the length needed.

Materials:
- *Ribbons*
- *Air-soluble marking pen*
- *Scissors*
- *Hand needle and thread*
- *Sewing machine, optional for some styles*

Straight-line Gathering

Stitch running stitches by hand or machine along one edge or down the center. Place narrow ribbon on top of wide ribbon for a layered ruffle effect. Stitch multiple rows for a shirred look. Longer stitches produce tighter gathers.

1. *Wire removed; gathered on long hand stitches.*

2. *Wire removed; gathered on short hand stitches.*

3. *Machine-gathered down center.*

4. *Layered, gathered.*

5. *Machine-gathered; three rows.*

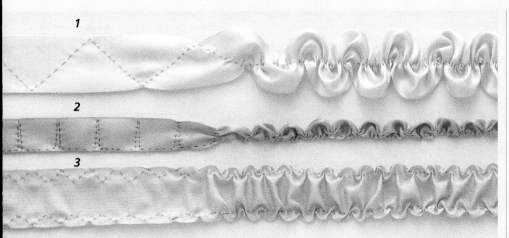

Patterned Gathering

Stitch running stitches in a marked pattern. Gather the ribbon to the desired fullness, arranging it evenly along the thread.

1. Serpentine: *Marks 2 RWs apart on each edge, staggered; wrap thread around selvage at each turn.*

2. Shell: *Marks 1 RW apart; wrap thread around selvage at points.*

3. Scallop: *Marks 1/2 RW apart; stitch zigzags 1/4 RW in from edge.*

Shell Smocking

1   Mark off both edges in 1-RW spaces. Mark center of the ribbon half-way between each of the outer marks.

2   Knot thread at first outer edge mark. Take small stitch in first center mark and another in opposite outer mark; pull three points together and knot.

3   Knot thread at the next outer mark, allowing it to lay flat between knots.

4   Repeat steps 2 and 3 down the ribbon to the desired length.

front

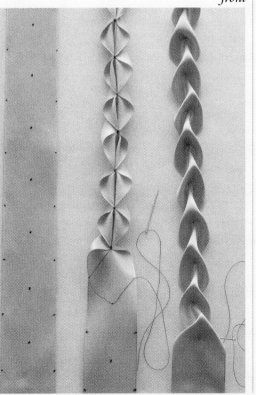

Lattice Smocking

1   Cut ribbon slightly longer than 1¼ times desired finished length of trim. Mark a grid of dots ¼" (6 mm) apart, centered on ribbon back, having an odd number of dots across.

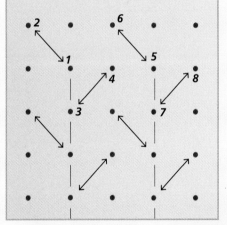

2   Knot thread at dot 1. Take a small stitch at dot 2; pull 1 and 2 together and knot. Knot thread at dot 3, allowing it to lay flat between knots. Take small stitch at dot 4; pull 3 and 4 together and knot.

3   Continue this pattern, working from side to side the length of the ribbon. Note that every other dot to the left and right of the column will be skipped.

4   Work the second column, following steps 2 and 3, beginning with dot 5, and taking stitches at dots that were omitted along right side of first column. Work remaining columns.

front

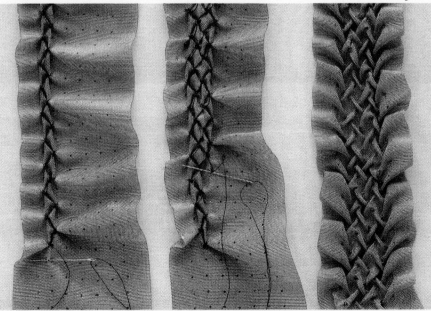

⪦ Ribbon Flowers ⪧

Ribbon flowers, both lifelike and fanciful, are made by gathering and manipulating lengths of ribbon. Similar techniques used on ribbons of different widths and colors can produce a variety of flowers that share characteristics but have their own distinctive looks. The leaves that accompany them and the materials used to create the centers of the flowers also help to distinguish one flower from another.

Almost any kind of ribbon can be used to make flowers. Some realistic looks result from using variegated and ombré ribbons. Ethereal, romantic looks can be achieved with sheer ribbons. Wired ribbons are suitable for many of the flowers, though removing the wire along the gathered edge helps to minimize bulk in the flower center. Wired outer edges of petals can be shaped and turned to give your flowers "attitudes."

Flowers that are intended to be sewn or glued to garments or accessories are tacked to a backing of stiff, woven interfacing as they are being formed. The excess backing is trimmed away when the flower is finished and doesn't show from the front. Flowers and leaves are then arranged and tacked to another piece of backing or secured directly to the item. Flowers that are intended to be freestanding in a vase or bouquet are attached to floral wire.

Materials:

- Ribbons
- Air-soluble marking pen
- Scissors
- Hand needle and thread
- Stiff, woven interfacing or crinoline
- Fray Check™
- Material for flower center (page 29)
- Floral wire; floral tape

Single Gathering Line
Open-end Method

1. Cut 5 to 15 RWs of ribbon, depending on the desired finished fullness. Remove wire from the inner edge (the edge that is to become the flower center). Apply Fray Check to the cut ends.

2. Thread the needle with double thread; knot the end. Insert the needle into the outer edge near the cut end; secure thread by running needle between the threads before pulling knot tight.

3. Stitch to the inner edge, round the corner, and stitch close to the inner edge the length of the ribbon. At the opposite end, round the corner and stitch to the outer edge.

4. Pull up on the thread, gathering the ribbon tightly. Knot the end to the beginning, turning raw edges to the back of the flower.

5. Tack the flower to a square of backing, directing short stitches from the center outward. Shape petals as desired and tack in place as needed along outer edges. Add a center to the flower, using one of the methods on page 29.

Closed Method

1 | Follow step 1 in open-end method. Stitch ends together in French seam, beginning at inner edge; knot. Stitch along inner edge, overlapping one stitch at the end.

2 | Pull up on thread, gathering ribbon tightly; tack to backing. Apply flower center.

Double Gathering Line

Using the closed method, stitch gathering lines along both edges to form buds, berries, and rose hips or to make calyxes for stemmed flowers. Stuff buds and berries with polyester fiberfill or beads.

1. Fanciful rosettes: *9 RWs of 3/8" to 7/8" (9 to 23 mm) ribbon; single, open-end method.*

2. Carnations: *9 to 11 RWs of 5/8" to 1 1/2" (15 to 39 mm) double-face ribbon; closed method, running the gathering line slightly off center. After gathering, fold layers so shorter petals are in middle.*

3. Petunia: *7 to 9 RWs of 1 1/2" or 2 1/4" (39 or 56 mm) ribbon; closed method, running a second gathering line 1/4 RW away from first. Gather the edge tight; gather the inner ring around the eraser end of a pencil, and knot.*

4. Poppy: *4 to 7 RWs per petal layer of 1 1/2" (39 mm) wire-edge ribbon; open-end method for multiple petals. Crimp the outer edge of the petals every 1/4" (6 mm) before gathering ribbon.*

5. Morning glory: *5 RWs of blue or purple wired ombré ribbon, 1 1/2" (39 mm) wide; closed method.*

Continuous-petal Flowers

Five-petal Flowers

1 Cut 12½ to 17½ RWs of ribbon, depending on the desired fullness. Remove wire from the inner edge (the edge that is to become the flower center). Apply Fray Check™ to the ends.

2 Mark off five equal spaces, 2½ to 3½ RWs wide, along the inner edge. Knot thread at the first mark. Stitch running stitches in the pattern shown, wrapping the thread around the outer edge at each mark.

3 Gather the ribbon tightly. Knot the end to the beginning, turning the raw edges to the back of the flower. Tack the flower to a square of backing. Apply flower center.

Serpentine Gathering

1 Mark off both edges of 1½ to 3 yd. (1.4 to 2.75 m) of ⅞" or 1½" (23 or 39 mm) ribbon into 2-RW segments, staggering the placement on opposite sides by 1 RW.

2 Knot thread at the first mark. Stitch diagonally in zigzag pattern, wrapping the thread around the outer edge at each mark.

3 Pull up thread, gathering ribbon to about one-fifth its original length.

4 Form tight circle with first three loops; tack to backing. Coil the remaining ribbon loosely around the center, tacking inner edges in place as you go. Turn under and tack ribbon end.

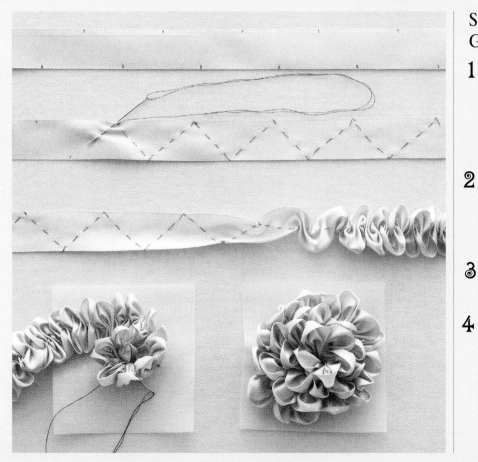

Looped Petals

1 Mark a ½" (1.3 cm) circle onto backing fabric. Cut 3 yd. (2.75 m) of ⅛" (3 mm) ribbon. Knot the thread near the end of the ribbon.

2 Take three small stitches into the ribbon 2" (5 cm) apart; pull up on thread, forming loops. Tack loops to circle, with loops pointing outward. Repeat, working around the circle.

3 Form an inner row of loops, as in step 2. Continue to ribbon end; tack end to backing.

1. **Forget-me-nots:** ⅝" (15 mm) blue ribbon; tiny pearl button with a black bead center.

2. **Camellia:** 50-RW length of ⅞" (23 mm) white ribbon; marked off in three 3-RW petals, four 4-RW petals, and five 5-RW petals. Gather and coil with smaller petals in the center.

3. **Buttercups:** ⅞" (23 mm) gold ombré wire-edge ribbon; yellow pompom for the center.

4. **Apple blossoms or wild roses:** ⅝" (15 mm) white or pink ribbon; artificial stamens for center.

5. **Zinnia:** 3 to 4 yd. (2.75 to 3.7 m) of 3/16" (5 mm) grosgrain ribbon; looped petals.

6. **Chrysanthemum or aster:** 3 to 5 yd. (2.75 to 4.6 m) of ⅛" (3 mm) satin or grosgrain ribbon; vary the size by varying the loop sizes.

7. **Dahlia:** 3 yd. (2.75 m) of 1½" (39 mm) satin ribbon; serpentine gathered.

Seam-shaped Petals

1 Cut ribbon to desired lengths for individual petals. Fold in half crosswise. Stitch a seam by hand or by machine, curving gradually from the petal base to the tip.

2 Apply Fray Check™ to both layers 1/8" (3 mm) from the seam; allow to dry. Trim seam allowance to 1/8" (3 mm).

3 Join petal bases with running stitches; overlap petals slightly for flowers with many single petals. Pull up thread to gather, joining petals into a circle.

4 Tack to backing or secure to stem wire. Apply flower center. Shape petals as desired.

Cut-shaped Petals

1 Mark off desired petal lengths on ribbon; apply Fray Check across at each mark, and allow to dry. Cut at marks; use pinking shears if desired, or shape petal ends in slight curves.

2 Join petal bases with running stitches; overlap petals slightly for flowers with many single petals. Pull up thread to gather, joining petals into a circle.

3 Tack to backing or secure to stem wire. Apply flower center. Shape petals as desired.

1. Dianthus: *Five 1" (2.5 cm) lengths of ⁷⁄₈" (23 mm) white ribbon, cut-shaped with pinking shears; bases tinted red with dye pen.*

2. Coneflower: *Ten to fifteen 2" to 4" (5 to 10 cm) lengths of pink 1¹⁄₂"*

(39 mm) wire ribbon, seam-shaped; coiled velvet cord center.

3. Daisy: *Fifteen 3¹⁄₂" (9 cm) lengths of ⁷⁄₈" (23 mm) white/yellow ombré wired ribbon, seam-shaped; frayed grosgrain ribbon center.*

4. Black-eyed Susan: *Fifteen 5" (12.7 cm) lengths of ⁷⁄₈" (23 mm) gold ombré wired ribbon, seam-shaped; coiled black velvet ribbon center.*

5. Coreopsis: *Eight 1¹⁄₂" (3.8 cm) lengths of ⁵⁄₈" (15 mm) yellow satin ribbon, cut-shaped with pinking shears; bases tined with red dye pen.*

6. Cosmos: *Ten 2" (5 cm) lengths of ¹⁄₂" (12 mm) pink ombré ribbon, cut-shaped with curved tips; frayed grosgrain ribbon center.*

7. Lily: *Six 5" to 7" (12.7 to 18 cm) lengths of 1¹⁄₂" or 2¹⁄₄" (39 or 56 mm) wired ribbons, seam-shaped; artificial stamens. Sword-shaped leaves are also made with the seam-shaped method.*

Roses

Wired Ribbon Rose

1 Cut ribbon: 16" (40.5 cm) of ⅝" (15 mm); 32" (81.5 cm) of 1½" (39 mm); or 1½ yd. (1.4 m) of 2¼" (56 mm). Bend a small loop in the end of a stem wire.

2 Pull out about 2" (5 cm) of wire on one edge of one end of ribbon; smooth ribbon flat. Fold 2" (5 cm) ribbon end down diagonally, then fold outer edge over. Slip the wire loop inside the folds. Wrap pulled wire around ribbon at bottom of folds, forming rose center.

3 Gather up remaining length of ribbon tightly, sliding ribbon along the same wire from the free end toward the rose center.

4 Wrap gathered edge around rose base, wrapping each layer slightly higher than the previous one. Fold the ribbon end down and catch under the last layer.

5 Wrap ribbon wire tightly around base to secure. Wrap floral tape around rose base, stretching tape and warming it with your fingers for best adhesion. Continue down stem, catching ribbon leaves as you wrap.

For a wired ribbon rose without a stem, omit the stem wire. Stitch the rose center, as formed in step 2, to the backing fabric. Work the gathered ribbon around the base, tacking it in place as you go.

Traditional Rose

1 Fold 2" (5 cm) ribbon end down diagonally, then fold outer edge over. Slip the wire loop inside the folds. Roll ribbon around base twice.

2 Fold ribbon back diagonally. Roll rose center over fold, keeping upper edge of rose center just below upper edge of fold. Roll to end of fold, forming a petal. Wrap tightly with floral wire.

3 Repeat step 2 until rose is desired size. Fold back ribbon end and secure to base. Wrap base with floral tape, continuing down stem wire.

For a traditional rose without a stem, omit the stem wire. Stitch the rose center to the backing fabric. Work the ribbon around the base, tacking it in place as you go.

Concertina Roses

1 Cut 12" (30.5 cm) of ⅜"or ½" (9 or 12 mm) ribbon. Fold under diagonally at the center, forming right angle. Turn the end that is underneath back over the center. Repeat with the other end.

2 Continue folding alternate ends back over previous folds, forming a square stack. Stop when the ends are 1" (2.5 cm) long.

3 Turn the stack over. Hold only the two ends, and release the stack. Holding ends securely, but loosely enough so they can slide, pull one end gently. A rose will form. Stop pulling when the excess ribbon is pulled out and the center of the rose sinks in. Tack to backing.

1. Wired ribbon rose wired to stem.

2. Wired ribbon roses sewn to backing fabric.

3. Traditional rose with leaf, wired to stem.

4. Traditional roses sewn to backing fabric.

5. Gathered roses made from extra-wide ribbon folded lengthwise; wired to stem or sewn to backing.

6. Concertina roses.

Combinations & Variations

Pansy: *Five 4-RW lengths of ⁷/₈" to 1¹/₂" (23 to 39 mm) variegated wire-edge ribbon; two sets of two, overlapped and gathered into double petals. Gather one piece on the dark side into a single petal. Gathering opposite edges of the double petals heightens contrast and creates the pansy's "face."*

Daffodil: *1¹/₂" (39 mm) gold ombré wired ribbon; 12-RW five-petal base, 6-RW double gathering line center cup. Make base. Gather bottom of cup; tack to base with ³/₈" (1 cm) radial stitches outward from center. Add flower stamens. Gather upper edge of cup.*

Peony: *2¹/₄" (56 mm) five-petal base; 3¹/₂" (89 mm) rosette center (page 19).*

Canterbury bells: *2¹/₂ RWs of 1¹/₂" (39 mm) blue ribbon; single gathering line, closed method (page 19) for flower base; scalloped gathering (page 17) for outer rim of bell.*

Leaves

Folded Leaf

1 | Cut a 3-RW length of ribbon. Fold ends down diagonally at the center; fold outer edges in.

2 | Pleat across the bottom, and twist tightly, if using wired ribbon. Or stitch running stitches across the bottom, catching the lower edge of the back; gather and knot.

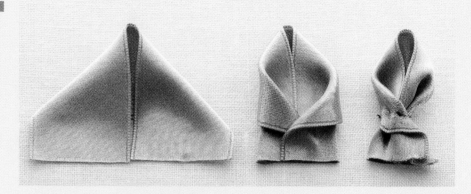

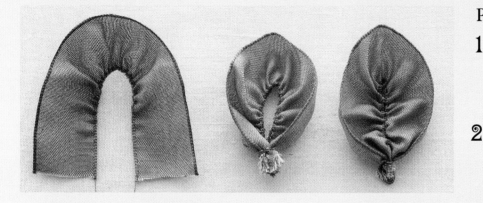

Pulled Wire Leaf

1 | Cut 6 RWs of wired ribbon. Pull up on wire from both ends of one side, gathering ribbon evenly toward center.

2 | Pleat across the bottom, and twist wire tightly around end. Glue or stitch gathered edges together in center of leaf.

Boat Leaf

1 | Cut 6- to 10-RW length of ribbon; fold in half crosswise. Fold ends up diagonally, to rest just below upper edge. Pin in place.

2 | Knot thread at one upper corner. Sew a running stitch down the diagonal fold, across the bottom of the "boat," and up the opposite diagonal fold.

3 | Gather to desired fullness; knot. Open leaf and adjust gathers.

Leaf/Calyx and Stem

Cut 6- to 10-RW length of wire-edge ribbon, depending on desired length of stem. Fold under right angle at center; then fold back over, aligning tails to form pointed leaf or calyx. Twist tails together below leaf to form stem.

Flower Centers

1. **French knots:** Use silk ribbon, embroidery floss, or other yarn.

2. **Artificial stamens:** Knot double thread around center of stamen cluster, or wrap floral wire around center, if making flowers with wired stems. Bend cluster in half; secure to flower center.

3. **Frayed grosgrain ribbon:** Cut one selvage from a length of grosgrain ribbon; fray the edge to within $1/8$" (3 mm) of other selvage. Roll from one end; secure to flower center.

4. **Ribbon knots:** Tie a small knot in a short piece of narrow ribbon. Pull tails through flower center, and secure to backing under flower.

5. **Coiled chenille stems:** Hand-tack or glue to flower center.

6. **Beaded stamens:** String bugle beads on fine craft wire for stamen, add seed bead or oat bead at end, and run wire back down through stamen. Repeat for multiple stamens; twist wires together and secure to flower center.

7. **Buttons:** Hand-stitch to flower center; catching seed bead over each hole.

Ribbon Embroidery

Silk ribbon embroidery can be used to adorn clothing and personal accessories or to embellish quilts or other home decor items. Beautiful in its own right, a silk ribbon embroidery piece deserves to be framed and displayed like other artwork. Narrow silk ribbons are sewn to fabric using a variety of unique stitches that create graceful, alluring curves and delicate dimensional designs. While some stitches used for ribbon embroidery are similar to those used for embroidering with finer threads, there are many special techniques that take advantage of the flat, pliable nature of silk ribbon. To establish a range of textures in a ribbon embroidery design, embroidery with various threads, beadwork, and other forms of needlework are often incorporated along with the ribbon embroidery.

Silk ribbons are available in various widths; 2 mm, 4 mm, and 7 mm are most commonly used for embroidery. The expansive color range includes solid colors, variegated colors, and sheers. Vivid jewel tones create a dynamic, contemporary look when used against a background equally as brilliant. Demure pastels are very soft and feminine, suitable for light-colored background fabrics. A vintage look can be created with muted, dusty tones embroidered on a background of antique linen or satin.

Needles

The types and sizes of needles used for ribbon embroidery depend on the ribbon width, the background fabric, and the stitch. Because these variables change throughout a project, keep on hand an assortment of sharp-pointed crewel needles, sizes 1 to 3, and chenille needles, sizes 18 to 24. The needle eye must be long enough to hold the full width of the ribbon and thick enough to create a hole large enough for the ribbon to easily slide through. Blunt-pointed tapestry needles are useful for stitches that pass between a previous stitch and the fabric, such as spider web roses (page 32) or the wrapping step of a whipped running stitch (opposite).

Marking Methods

Embroidery patterns can be transferred to fabric, using various marking pens and pencils. Because the embroidery may not cover all the marks completely, avoid any permanent markings. Water-soluble or air-soluble markers are useful on light-colored fabrics. Keep in mind, however, that air-soluble marks disappear in twelve hours. Silver or white quilt marking pencils work well on bright or dark fabrics and are easily removed or covered.

To transfer the pattern to the fabric, layer the fabric, right side up, over the pattern, over a light box. A sunny window or a light placed under a glass-top table work just as well. Or trace the pattern on sheer netting and transfer the pattern to the fabric through the netting.

Preparing the Fabric

Many fabrics are suitable backgrounds for ribbon embroidery. The fabric should be compatible with the look and feel of the design and the intended use. Whenever possible, the fabric should be held taut in an embroidery hoop or needlework frame. This prevents the stitches from puckering the fabric and helps you develop a consistent stitch tension. To prevent the hoop from imprinting the fabric, wrap the inner hoop with twill tape or yarn.

Threading & Knotting the Ribbon

1 Thread an 18" (46 cm) length of ribbon through the eye of the needle. Pierce the center of the ribbon 1/4" (6 mm) from the threaded end; pull the long end of the ribbon, locking the ribbon on the needle eye.

2 Fold over the free end of the ribbon 1/4" (6 mm), and pierce the center of both layers with the needle. Draw the needle and ribbon through, forming a soft knot at the ribbon end.

Ending

End the ribbon by running the needle to the underside of the fabric; draw the ribbon across the nearest stitch. Piercing both layers, take two small stitches to lock the ribbon. Trim off the ribbon tail.

Stitches

Straight Stitch

Come up at 1 and go down at 2, the desired distance away; keep the ribbon flat. Make running stitches by continuing in a straight line, with small spaces between stitches. Make straight stitches that radiate from a single point to create a flower or bud.

Whip Stitch

Make a single straight stitch. Bring the needle back up through the fabric at the base of the straight stitch. Wrap the ribbon around the stitch two or three times, keeping the ribbon flat. Go back down in the fabric at the opposite end of the stitch.

Whipped Running Stitch

Stitch a line of running stitches. Thread ribbon onto a blunt needle. Come up through the fabric at the first stitch. Wrap each stitch twice, keeping the ribbon flat. Proceed to each succeeding stitch to the end of the line before returning to the back of the fabric.

Ribbon Stitch

Come up at 1. Smooth the ribbon flat in the direction of the stitch. Insert the needle at the end of the stitch 2, piercing the center of the ribbon. Pull the needle through to the underside until the ribbon curls inward at the tip. Take care not to pull the ribbon too tight.

Lazy Daisy

Bring the needle up from the underside at the petal base; insert the needle right next to the exit point, and bring the needle back up at the petal tip. Pull the ribbon through the fabric, forming a small, smooth loop. Pass the ribbon over the loop; secure it with a small straight stitch at the tip.

Filled Lazy Daisy

Make a lazy daisy stitch (above). Using another color of ribbon, make a straight stitch from the base of the lazy daisy to just below the tip.

Loop Stitch

Bring the needle up from the underside; pull ribbon through. Loop the ribbon smoothly over a holder, such as a trolley needle or large plastic darning needle held in the hand opposite the hand that holds the needle. Insert the needle into the fabric right in front of the exit point. Pull the ribbon through the fabric until the loop tightens around the holder. Continue to hold the completed loop until the next stitch is taken.

Work five loop stitches in a circle to make a flower. Work several French knots or colonial knots (page 33) in the center.

Plume Stitch

Bring the needle up through the fabric. Stitch back down, about ⅛" (3 mm) below the first hole. Pull the ribbon through the fabric until the loop tightens around a holder, such as a trolley needle, plastic straw, or large plastic darning needle held in the nonstitching hand. Bring the needle back up through the fabric, piercing the base of the previous loop; pull the ribbon through before removing the holder. Repeat to the desired length of the plume.

Stem Stitch

Bring the needle up through the fabric at the start of the marked or imaginary stem; make a small straight stitch. Bring the needle back through the fabric partway back and alongside the previous stitch. Repeat continuously for the desired length; keep the ribbon smooth without twisting.

Chain Stitch

Bring the needle up through the fabric at the beginning of a marked or imaginary line. Form a loop, and insert the needle next to, but not in, the first hole; bring the needle back out forward on the line, with the needle going over the ribbon. Pull up on the ribbon. Repeat the stitch to the desired line length.

Coral Stitch

1 Bring the needle and ribbon up through the fabric at the starting point. Smooth the ribbon flat along the marked or imaginary line. Make a gentle arch and hold the ribbon in place.

2 Take a tiny stitch under the ribbon arch; pass the needle over the ribbon tail while pulling ribbon through fabric. Gradually release ribbon arch, forming a soft knot. Continue along marked or imaginary line; vary distance between knots and flatten or raise segments as desired.

Spider Web Rose

1 Draw a circle with five evenly spaced spokes. Using embroidery floss or other fine cord, form a stitch along each of the spokes and tie off.

2 Bring the ribbon up at the center of the web. Weave the ribbon over and under the spokes in a circular fashion, working gradually outward, until the spokes are covered and the desired fullness is achieved. Keep the ribbon loose; twists in the ribbon add interest. Push the needle through to the back and secure.

Couching

1 Thread first needle with ribbon to be couched; thread second needle with narrower ribbon or thread that will hold first one in place. Bring first needle up through fabric. Smooth ribbon toward nonstitching hand; hold under thumb on desired path.

2 Bring second needle up through fabric at first couching point, just below ribbon. Take small stitch over wider ribbon. Repeat to end.

3 Pass first needle back through fabric at the end of path; secure ribbon. Secure couching ribbon or thread at last couching point.

Bead Couching

Follow directions for couching (above), using beading needle for second needle. Secure seed bead at each couching point. Allow ribbon to twist and turn along line, if desired.

Fly Stitch

Bring needle up at 1 and down at 2; keep ribbon flat and loose. Come up below and half-way between two points, with ribbon below needle. Pull through, forming V. Insert needle just below point of V to secure. Repeat stitches in a column, narrowing toward the top, to create a stacked fly stitch.

Feather Stitch

Follow directions for fly stitch; begin at top of intended line, but don't secure stitch. Repeat, alternating from left to right. Secure last stitch.

French Knot

Bring needle up from underside. Holding needle parallel to fabric near exit point, wrap ribbon once or twice around needle; take care to keep ribbon smooth. Insert needle very close to exit point, holding ribbon in place close to wrapped needle. Hold ribbon while pulling needle through to underside, releasing ribbon as it disappears. Ribbon forms soft knot.

Colonial Knot

Bring needle up through fabric. Form clockwise loop with ribbon and slide needle tip under it. Then wrap ribbon back over and under needle in figure 8. Insert needle back into fabric very near first hole; pull ribbon loosely around needle while drawing needle to back of fabric.

Imperial Rose

Bring needle and ribbon up through fabric. Pierce ribbon 1" to 1½" (2.5 to 3.8 cm) above surface; stitch ¼" (6 mm) running stitches in ribbon to just above surface. Insert needle back to underside near first hole. Draw ribbon through gently, stacking folds. Stop when upper fold begins to curl inward.

Designer Projects

Nancy Overton

As a professional designer and new product manager, Nancy Overton has 20 years of experience in developing innovative products for the craft and gift markets. She is an expert at taking creative concepts and turning them into practical designs for manufacturers or realistic projects for consumer publications. Her ribbon craft designs are among her favorites.

Boudoir Ensemble

Delicate ribbon embroidery stitches have been worked into a lovely trailing design for the front banding on a ready-to-wear silky bed jacket. A similar pattern is embroidered in a circle on the front of a dreamy blue chenille pillow. Motifs from the design are repeated on sachets to be hung in the closet or over a bedpost or tucked into drawers.

The only tricky part of working this design on the bed jacket is keeping the stitches hidden between the layers of the banding. Nancy suggests that you begin and end the embroidery on the right side of the garment, where knots can be hidden under other stitches. Gently work the needle between the fabric layers to travel from one stitch to another.

Ribbons:

- *Cream silk ribbon, 4 mm*
- *Light pink silk ribbon, 4 mm*
- *Deep coral silk ribbon, 4 mm*
- *Pale grass silk ribbon, 4 mm*
- *Forest green silk ribbon, 4 mm*

Other Materials:

- *Ready-to-wear bed jacket with neckline and front banding*
- *Fabric and filling for 18" to 20" (46 to 51 cm) pillow, or ready-made pillow*
- *Fabrics for sachets; potpourri*
- *Pink embroidery floss*

Sachets

1. Mark two 5" (12.7 cm) squares on sachet fabric. Mark design in center of one square; embroider.

2. Cut out the squares. If hanger is desired, pin 9" (23 cm) length of ribbon along upper edge of embroidered square, with ends 1" (2.5 cm) from corners. Pin squares right sides together.

3. Stitch ½" (1.3 cm) seam around square, taking care not to catch hanger in stitches, and leaving 1½" (3.8 cm) opening on one side.

4. Trim corners. Turn right side out. Fill with potpourri. Stitch opening closed.

Pillow

1. Mark the placement of the roses and daisies around an 8¼" (21.2 cm) circle. Stitch the spider web roses with pink floss and light pink and deep coral ribbon. Make the leaves around the light pink roses, using forest green lazy daisy stitches; use pale grass green for the coral roses.

2. Stitch the daisy petals with cream lazy daisy stitches; stitch the daisy centers with three pale grass green French knots.

3. Stitch pale grass green feather stitch to fill in between the flowers, alternating the arms of the stitch to the left and right of the circle.

4. Stitch partial daisies with cream ribbon stitch; fill in with white and light pink French knots.

Bed Jacket

1. Mark the locations of the spider web roses and daisies, using air-soluble pen. Stitch the spider web roses with three-ply pink embroidery floss and light pink silk ribbon. Make the leaves, using forest green lazy daisy stitches.

2. Stitch the daisy petals with cream lazy daisy stitches.

3. Fill in between the flowers with pale grass green feather stitches. Add cream French knots.

Stitch Key

- Spider Web Rose
- Lazy Daisy
- Ribbon Stitch
- Feather Stitch
- French Knot

Pillow

Bed Jacket

Sachets

(right)

(left)

(middle)

Janis Bullis

"Helping consumers enjoy the benefits and rewards of creative sewing and crafts" is Janis Bullis's professional goal. She has served the home decorating, apparel, and craft industries for more than 25 years as a consultant and designer, with clients that include book, magazine, and pattern publishers.

Braided Ribbon Clothing Details

Janis Bullis uses braided ribbon trims to add snappy character and individual style to ordinary clothing. A simple, collarless, red linen jacket makes a unique fashion statement with the addition of braided ribbon trims on the sleeves and welt pockets. A simple pattern with one-piece sleeves works best; complete instructions for the welt pockets are given on pages 42 and 43, so they need not be included in the pattern you select.

A basic, empire-waist, satin evening gown is given a one-of-a-kind look with braided ribbon trims. Rolled three-ply braids (page 12) are used for the spaghetti straps. Two-tone loop braids (page 13) gracefully crisscross the back and cascade to calf-length amid streamers of feather-edge and plain, double-face, satin ribbons. These ribbon trims can be used to transform a simple purchased gown or incorporated into a custom-sewn gown.

Jacket Accents

Ribbons:

- 1⅝ yd. (1.5 m) jade, single-face satin ribbon, ¼" (7 mm) wide
- 1 yd. (0.92 m) jade, single-face satin ribbon, ⅜" (9 mm) wide
- 1 yd. (0.92 m) jade, single-face satin ribbon, ⅝" (15 mm) wide
- 7½ yd. (6.9 m) red, single-face satin ribbon, ¹⁄₁₆" (1.5 mm) wide
- 2½ yd. (2.3 m) red, single-face satin ribbon, ⅛" (3 mm) wide
- Red, single-face satin ribbon, 2¼" (56 mm) wide, for covering button, optional

Other Materials:

- Jacket pattern
- Fabric and lining
- Notions
- ⅞" (2.2 cm) button
- Sewing machine

Artist's Tip: *Select ribbon colors to suit your fabric choice. Match the braiding ribbon to the jacket fabric and underlay the braid with a ribbon color that makes it stand out. Layering a warm color over a cool color (or vice versa) makes the trim more apparent. True complementary colors of the same intensity may tend to "vibrate." Analogous colors may blend together and produce a more subtle effect. Try various combinations before you buy.*

Sleeves

1 Before sewing the sleeves, mark placement lines for the ⅝" (15 mm) jade ribbon on the sleeve pieces 1½" (3.8 cm) above and parallel to the hemline. Stitch ribbon in place along both edges, extending the ribbon into the seam allowances.

2 Stitch the ⅜" and ¼" (9 and 7 mm) jade ribbons above the wide ribbon, leaving ½" (1.3 cm) spaces between them.

3 Following the instructions for flat three-ply braiding (page 12), braid three lengths of ⅛" (3 mm) red ribbon. Center the braid over the wide jade ribbon; hand-tack in place. Repeat for the narrower jade ribbons, using ¹⁄₁₆" (1.5 mm) red ribbons for the braid. Follow pattern instructions for sewing the sleeves.

Pockets

1 Cut four pocket lining pieces, each 7" × 8" (18 × 20.5 cm). Cut four welt pieces from jacket fabric, each 7" × 3⅝" (18 × 9.3 cm). Cut four 6" (15 cm) lengths of ¼" (7 mm) jade ribbon. Cut twelve 7" (18 cm) lengths of ¹⁄₁₆" (1.5 mm) red ribbon.

2 Draw a rectangle on the pocket lining 5" × ⅝" (12.7 × 1.5 cm), centering it 1½" (3.8 cm) from one short end and two long sides. Pin the lining to the right side of the jacket over the pocket location; stitch around the rectangle. Cut through all layers through the rectangle center, stopping ¼" (6 mm) from the ends. Clip diagonally up to, but not through, the four corners.

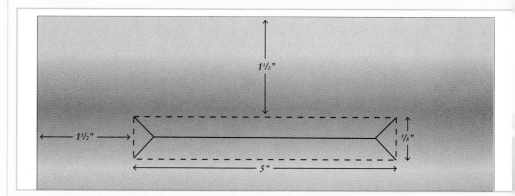

3 Push lining through the opening to the wrong side; press flat, creating a clean finished opening with sharp corners. Repeat for remaining pocket.

4 Place two welt pieces, right sides together. Mark the lengthwise center; machine baste together. Press welts right sides out, with basted seam in the center and open edges outward. Repeat for remaining welt.

5 Stitch ¼" (7 mm) jade ribbon strips on either side of and close to the basted seam. Braid ¹⁄₁₆" (1.5 mm) ribbons; hand-tack to centers of jade ribbons.

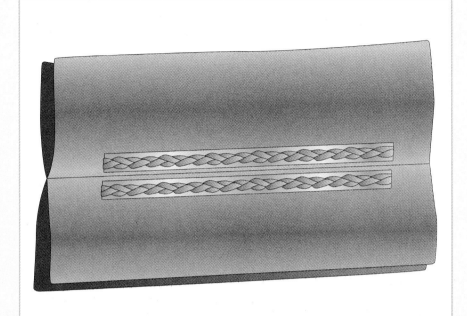

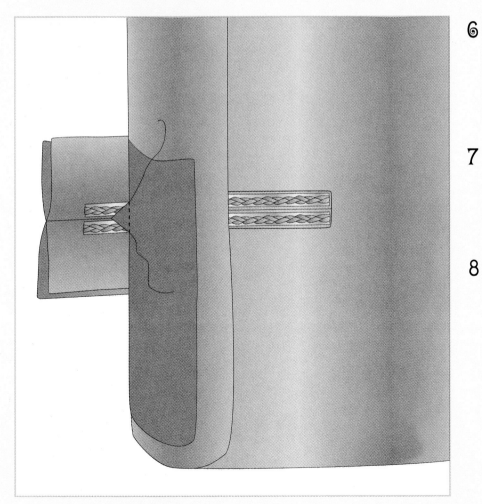

6 Center the welt piece under the opening. Working on one side at a time, roll back the jacket and pocket lining, exposing the seam allowances of the opening; stitch over the existing stitching lines.

7 Pin the remaining pocket lining pieces to the welted lining pieces. Stitch around the outer edge through lining pieces only. Remove basting stitches of welt seam.

8 Finish sewing the jacket, following the pattern instructions. Cover any buttons, using the wide red ribbon.

Woven Ribbon & Lattice-trimmed Garments

by Janis Bullis

Woven ribbon fabric adds pizzazz to a blazer, turning it from everyday conservative to party perfect. Janis chose a variety of ribbons in coordinating colors and styles and wove them together in a plain weave to create the "designer fabric" for the patch pockets and notched lapels of her jacket. Follow the weaving techniques on pages 10 and 11, using any of the weave patterns to create your ribbon fabric. Simply substitute the ribbon fabric for the garment fabric in constructing the blazer, following the pattern grainlines.

Narrow satin ribbons are delicately held in place with pearl beads in a lattice design over the yokes of this shantung blouse. The ribbons are arranged over the yoke pieces before constructing the blouse. Spaced 2" (5 cm) apart and at 45° angles to the fabric grainline, they are secured at each intersection and in the seam allowances around the outer edges.

Sandra McCooey

It is Sandra McCooey's belief that if people just tried ribbon embroidery, they would fall in love with it, just as she did. "It is so romantic and easy." Her passion for ribbon embroidery has led her to create many original designs that even beginners can complete successfully.

Straw Handbag & Shoes

Mesh shoes and a straw handbag
take on designer flair when
they are embellished with this
original silk ribbon design. The tiny
roses flanking the large spider
web rose are a stitch that Sandra
learned from a woman in Japan. She
calls it the "imperial rose."
A chenille needle is recommended
for this project, to avoid
breaking or splitting the fibers
in the handbag.

Ribbons:
- *Mauve pink silk ribbon, 13 mm*
- *Mauve silk ribbon, 7 mm*
- *Dusty purple silk ribbon, 4 mm*
- *Jungle green silk ribbon, 4 mm*

Other Materials:
- *Pink embroidery floss*
- *Straw handbag*
- *Straw or mesh shoes*
- *Chenille needle*

Handbag

1. Remove the lining from inside the bag. Save it to replace later, or make a new lining to match the ribbon colors. Mark the placement of the main design elements, using air-soluble marking pen.

2. Stitch the spider web rose, using the pink floss for the spokes and weaving the rose with the 13 mm mauve pink ribbon.

3. Stitch the straight stitches with the purple ribbon; stitch the lazy daisy stitches with the green ribbon.

4. Stitch the imperial roses with the 7 mm mauve ribbon, taking care not to pull them too tightly.

5. Replace the lining.

Handbag

Shoes

1 Stitch the design, using the same ribbons and stitches as for the handbag.

2 Stitch two imperial roses at the back of each shoe. Add three green straight stitches in a fan shape under the roses. (not shown)

Right Shoe

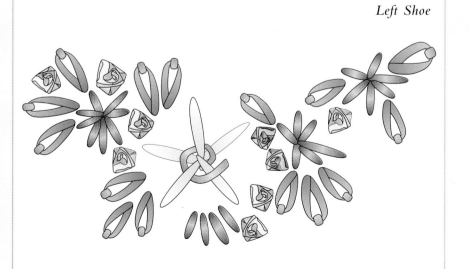

Left Shoe

Stitch Key

- Straight Stitch
- Spider Web Rose
- Lazy Daisy
- Imperial Rose

Baby Ensemble

by Nancy Overton

Welcome a precious baby to the
world with an adorably cuddlesome
blanket that features a
blanket-stitched fleece bunny and a
silk ribbon embroidered
binding, celebrating the day of birth.
With a few simple embroidery
stitches and a pleated ribbon
trim, turn an ordinary body suit and
cap into a designer outfit.

⇜ Baby Ensemble ⇝

Ribbons:
- Dark coral or robin egg blue silk ribbon, 4 mm
- Yellow silk ribbon, 4 mm
- Dark coral or robin egg blue silk ribbon, 7 mm
- Pale grass green silk ribbon, 4 mm
- Pink or blue satin ribbon, ⅜" (9 mm)

Other Materials:
- Fleece baby blanket with satin binding
- 7" × 10" (18 × 25.5 cm) piece of fleece or polyester felt
- Infant's knit body suit and cap
- Pink or blue embroidery floss
- Light green embroidery floss
- Tracing paper
- Netting
- Dressmaker's chalk or removable marker

Artist's Tip: *Nancy advises that designs need not be replicated exactly to be pleasing to the eye. On some fabrics, like fleece, felt, and the chenille pillow on page 37, transferring marks is not practical. Instead, she suggests marking key design elements with pins and working them first. Then fill in the spaces with secondary elements. Feel free to ad-lib a little!*

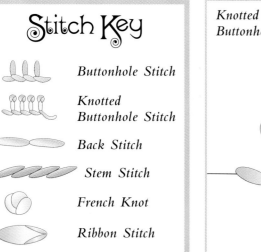

Stitch Key
- Buttonhole Stitch
- Knotted Buttonhole Stitch
- Back Stitch
- Stem Stitch
- French Knot
- Ribbon Stitch

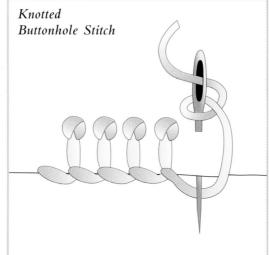

Knotted Buttonhole Stitch

Body Suit and Cap

1 Trace the heart patterns on tracing paper, and cut them out. Cut out fleece hearts.

2 Make yellow French knots for the flower centers. Make coral or blue ribbon stitch petals.

3 Pin the hearts to the clothes. Using three strands of pink or blue embroidery floss, attach the hearts with knotted buttonhole stitches, spaced about 3/16" (4.5 mm) apart.

4 Pleat 3/8" (9 mm) pink or blue satin ribbon into bow-tie trim (page 15). Secure trim to waistline seam of body suit by stitching yellow French knots through all layers at the center of each bow tie. Open the side seams, and restitch them, catching the ribbon ends in the seams.

Body Suit

Cap

Blanket

1. Trace the bunny pattern on tracing paper, and cut it out. Cut out a fleece bunny. Using the pattern as a guide, mark the flower center with a pin.

2. Make three French knots for the flower center, using yellow ribbon. Make six ribbon stitch flower petals radiating from the center, using coral or blue 7 mm ribbon.

3. Make a slightly curved line of stem stitches on each side of the flower, using green silk ribbon. Make green ribbon stitch leaves originating from alternating sides of the stems.

4. Using three strands of pink or blue floss, make a French knot for the bunny's eye.

Bunny

5 Cut a 1¹/₂" (3.8 cm) piece of coral or blue 7 mm silk ribbon for the bunny's collar. Pin it to the bunny's neck with ends tucked to the back of the fabric. Using three strands of pink or blue embroidery floss, make French knots to secure the collar, catching the ends with the first and last knots.

6 Using your own script or printing, letter the baby's name and birth date on a ruled line on a piece of netting. Leave room between the name and date for a ribbon flower. Transfer the letters to the blanket, by tracing through the netting with a chalk dressmaker's pencil or removable marker.

7 Using three strands of pink or blue embroidery floss, embroider the letters, using the backstitch. Embroider the flower center with yellow French knots; use 7 mm ribbon for the ribbon stitch petals.

8 Pin the bunny to the blanket. Using three strands of pink or blue embroidery floss, attach the bunny with buttonhole stitches, spaced about ³/₁₆" (4.5 mm) apart.

9 Stitch the French knots in the lower right corner of the blanket, using yellow and coral or blue ribbon. Make the stem stitches, using three strands of green embroidery floss. Make green ribbon stitch leaves originating from alternating sides of the stems.

10 Cut a 24" to 30" (61 to 76 cm) length of coral or blue 7 mm silk ribbon. Thread the ribbon onto a needle and take a small stitch under the corner flower stems; pull the ribbon through. Tie a small bow over the stems, leaving a longer tail to trail under the letters. Couch the tails to the binding, using silk ribbon French knots; allow the tails to turn and twist gracefully.

Flower

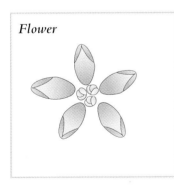

Buttonhole Stitch

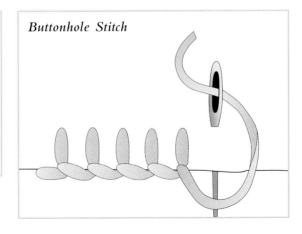

Backstitch

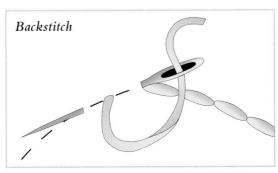

Pansy-trimmed Evening Bag & Beret

by Nancy Overton

A simple black velvet evening bag and

beret become saucy accessories

with the addition of a few pert pansies.

Well-suited to the task, ombré ribbons in shades

of purple and pink, or any other pansy

color, make pansies so true to life, one must

touch them to know for sure.

Pansies and Leaves

Follow the instructions on page 27 for making
pansies, gauging the amount of ribbon needed by the
number of pansies and ribbon widths used for each.
Finish the pansies with knotted ribbon centers,
and make folded leaves to accompany them (page 28).
Hand-tack or glue pansies to a purchased handbag
and beret. Make a snappy lapel pin simply by gluing
a pansy to a 1⅝" (4 cm) jewelry pin back.

Markena Lanska

The endless possibilities for design and the sheer joy of working with ribbons captured Markena Lanska's attention long ago. Her imagination is always working and her hands are always busy creating new ribbon manipulation and ribbon embroidery projects for juried gallery events, magazine articles, and book publications.

Spectacular Straw Hats

A modest straw hat becomes a fetching

fashion statement with

the addition of a fancy ribbon

hatband. Choose a removable headband

style, featuring three five-petal

gathered flowers over a gathered ribbon

base. Or make a more elaborate

embroidered and beaded

hatband, a testament to your love

of ribbon work.

Ribbons:

- *"Candelabra" wire-edge nubby linen ribbon by Morex Corp., 1½" (39 mm) wide in antique white, beige, and sage green*

Other Materials:

- *Straw hat*
- *Headband*
- *FabriTac® glue*

Headband-style Hatband

1 Measure the curve length of the headband. Cut beige ribbon three times this length. Stitch two rows of gathering stitches, about ½" (1.3 cm) apart, down the center of the ribbon; knot the thread securely at the start, and leave short tails at the ends.

2 Pull out the wires a short distance at the knotted ends; twist the wires together. Slide the ribbon toward the knotted end on the wires and gathering stitches, until the piece is the same length as the headband curve; adjust the gathers evenly.

3 Tie off the gathering threads and twist the wires together at the other end; trim off excess wire and thread. Glue the gathered ribbon to the headband, tucking the raw ends under; set aside.

4 Cut three 18" (46 cm) pieces of antique white ribbon. Remove the wire from one edge of each. Make five-petal flowers, using the continuous petal method on page 20.

5 Make ribbon knot centers (page 29) for the flowers, using 6" (15 cm) of the beige ribbon for each. Glue flowers to center arch of headband.

6 Make two pulled-wire leaves (page 28), using 6" (15 cm) of sage green ribbon for each. Glue to headband at opposite ends of the flowers.

7 Slip the headband onto the hat, hugging the base of the crown. Or wear it as a headband.

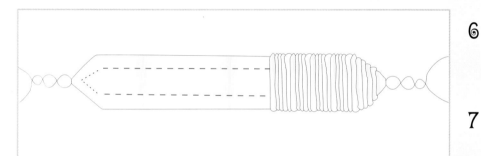

Ribbons:

- 1¼ yd. (1.15 m) dark blue wire-edge or grosgrain ribbon, 2¼" (56 mm) wide
- Light coral silk ribbon, 4 mm
- Deep salmon silk ribbon, 4 mm
- Pale hunter green silk ribbon, 4 mm

Other Materials:

- Straw hat
- Pale pink and medium green embroidery floss
- Water-soluble stabilizer, such as Solvy®
- Ballpoint pen

Optional Beading Materials:

- Beads: matte gold, green, mixture of pinks
- Beading thread
- Size 11 sharp or appliqué needles
- Thread conditioner

Embroidered and Beaded Hatband

1 Cut a length of wide blue ribbon the measurement around the crown of the hat plus 3" (7.5 cm). Cut 2¼" (6 cm) strip of water-soluble stabilizer the same length. Trace the hatband embroidery pattern (page 63) onto the stabilizer, using ballpoint pen; start and end about 2" (5 cm) from the cut ends.

2 Cut 18" (46 cm) of wide ribbon for the bow. Cut two 4" (10 cm) strips of stabilizer; trace the pattern for the bow embroidery (page 63) on the stabilizer. Baste to ribbon, starting pattern 5" (12.7 cm) from cut ends; flip one piece so pattern will be reverse image.

3 Embroider the stems with stem stitch, using two strands of green embroidery floss.

4 Embroider the six-petal flowers with loop stitches, using light coral silk ribbon.

5 Embroider the spokes of the spider web roses, using pink floss. Weave the center half of the roses, using light coral silk ribbon; finish the outer half with salmon silk ribbon.

(continued)

Embroidered and Beaded Hatband *(continued)*

6 Embroidery the rosebuds with padded straight stitches (a short straight stitch covered by a longer straight stitch), using light coral and salmon silk ribbons in random placement. Embroider a calyx for each rosebud with straight stitches, using pale hunter green silk ribbon.

7 Embroider the small leaves with ribbon stitches, using pale hunter green silk ribbon. Embroider the large leaves with straight stitches laid side by side, using pale hunter green; use the ribbon stitch for the leaf tips.

8 Embroider leaf buds at the ends of the stems with colonial knots, using pale hunter green silk ribbon, to complete the embroidery.

9 Thread a size 11 sharp needle with a double strand of beading thread; apply thread conditioner to lessen tangles. Stitch seven matte gold seed beads in the centers of the loop flowers: one in the center and one at the base of each petal.

Artist's Tip: Markena suggests that beginning stitchers may wish to stop at this point and finish the hat. Intermediate or advanced stitchers may wish to continue embellishing the ribbon embroidery with more beads.

10 Using green seed beads, stitch a bead to the base of each small leaf; stitch a bead to the base of each bud calyx. Stitch one bead on top of each colonial knot. Stitch a line of beads down the center of each large leaf, passing the needle through all the beads at once; pass the needle and thread through a second time to secure the line.

11 Using a mix of pink seed beads, stitch a bead at the base of each pink bud. Embellish the spider web roses with a scattering of single transparent pink beads near the center; stitch lines of mixed pink beads to emphasize the outer folds.

Artist's Tip: When you finish embroidering and beading the ribbon, plunge it into cold water to dissolve the stabilizer. Swish it gently and rinse in clear water. Then secure the ribbons to a fan with a clothespin. This will dry and puff out the ribbon.

12 To finish, wrap the hatband around the crown of the hat, overlapping in the back; hand-tack in several locations to secure.

13 Fold under the plain ribbon ends of the bow, overlapping the cut ends. Cut a 4" (10 cm) piece of ribbon for the bow center. Fold a gentle pleat in the ribbon and wrap it around the bow, overlapping cut ends in the back. Hand-tack all ends in place. Glue or stitch the bow over the center back of the hatband.

Hatband

Bow

5"
(12.7 cm)
from the
cut edge

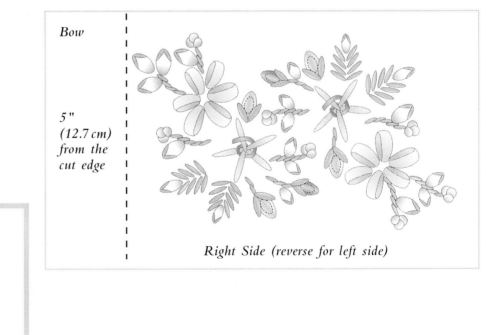

Right Side (reverse for left side)

Stitch Key

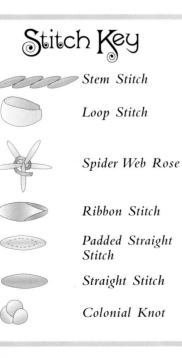

Stem Stitch

Loop Stitch

Spider Web Rose

Ribbon Stitch

Padded Straight Stitch

Straight Stitch

Colonial Knot

Ribbon Hair Accessories

by Markena Lanska

Hair accessories fit for a
princess are designed by Markena
Lanska. She has incorporated
a variety of techniques that involve
ribbon manipulation and
silk ribbon embroidery. The combs
and barrettes are quick to whip up,
perhaps using ribbon leftovers
from some of your other projects.
The embroidered headband
would be a lovely crowning touch
for a special celebration
in a young girl's life. With a selective
choice of ribbon styles and
colors, any of these accessories are
suitable for girls of any age.

Beaded Rosettes
Barrette Ribbons:

- *13 mm silk ribbons or ⅝" (15 mm) single-face satin ribbons, in desired flower and leaf colors*

Other Materials:

- *Scrap of white silk*
- *3" (7.5 cm) metal barrette*
- *Press-on Score and Break Plastic*
- *Fray Check™*
- *Four 8 mm faceted crystal beads*
- *Needle and thread*
- *Embroidery hoop*
- *FabriTac™ glue*

Beaded Rosettes Barrette

1. Cut ¾" × 3" (2 × 7.5 cm) rectangle of plastic. Mark ¾" × 3" (2 × 7.5 cm) rectangle on silk, using removable marker; place silk in hoop.

2. Make four rosettes, using 4" (10 cm) of ribbon for each, with closed gathering method (page 19). Hand-tack, evenly spaced, down center of silk. Stitch a crystal bead to the center of each flower.

3. Make ten folded leaves (page 28). Hand-tack five leaves on each side of the flowers, hiding the ends under the flowers. Angle leaf rows in opposite directions.

4. Remove fabric from hoop. Remove protective backing from plastic board; adhere board to back of silk rectangle. Trim fabric to within ½" (1.3 cm) of board. Fold and glue the raw edges to the back of the board; glue board to barrette.

Metallic Roses
Barrette Ribbons:

- *Green metallic ribbon, ⅛" (3 mm) wide, for leaves*
- *⅔ yd. (0.63 m) silver grosgrain ribbon, ⅜" (9 mm) wide, for concertina roses*
- *⅔ yd. (0.63 m) silver double-faced satin ribbon, ⅝" (15 mm) wide, for gathered rosettes*

Other Materials:

- *White silk, about 6" × 6" (15 × 15 cm)*
- *Silver-gray sewing thread; needle*
- *Press-on Score and Break Plastic, 1" × 2½" (2.5 × 6.5 cm)*
- *2" (5 cm) metal barrette*
- *Embroidery hoop*
- *FabriTac glue*

Metallic Roses Barrette

1. Mark outline of pastic base in center of silk, using removable marker; mark placement of flowers and leaves. Put fabric in small hoop.

2. Stitch the leaves with multiple straight stitches for each.

3. Make two concertina roses (page 25), using 12" (30.5 cm) silver grosgrain ribbon for each. Secure to the silk, following the placement guide.

4. Cut satin ribbon into six 4" (10 cm) pieces. Using the closed method, single gathering line (page 19), make three rosettes with the gathering line stitched along one edge. Tack them to the silk, following the placement guide. With the three remaining pieces, using the closed method, center the gathering line to make double-ruffle rosettes. Tack them to the centers of the single rosettes.

5. Remove fabric from hoop. Remove protective backing from plastic board; adhere board to back of silk rectangle. Trim fabric to within ½" (1.3 cm) of board. Fold and glue the raw edges to the back of the board; glue board to barrette.

Metallic Roses

Gathered Rose
Hair Comb Ribbons:
- *3 yd. (2.75 m) sheer wire-edge ribbon, 1" (25 mm) wide*
- *⅔ yd. (0.63 m) moss green wire-edge ribbon, 1" (25 mm) wide*

Other Materials:
- *Hair comb, 3" (7.5 cm) wide*
- *FabriTac glue*

Gathered Rose Hair Comb

1 | Make two folded leaves (page 28), using 6" (15 cm) of green ribbon for each.

2 | Ease the wire ends out of one end of a 1 yd. (0.92 m) length of the sheer ribbon; twist them together. Pulling from the other end, gather the ribbon tightly along the bottom wire; gather very loosely on the top wire. Twist the wire ends together.

3 | Accordion-fold the ribbon; hand-tack layers together at the center bottom, forming a bud. Crush the bud in your palms.

4 | Repeat steps 2 and 3 to make a second bud. Wrap a 6" (15 cm) length of green ribbon around the base of each bud as if forming another folded leaf. Wrap calyx and bud together with ribbon wire; wrap leaf and bud together.

5 | Make a wired ribbon rose (page 24), using a 2 yd. (1.85 m) length of the sheer ribbon. Glue buds to ends of comb heading, pointing in opposite directions. Glue rose to center of comb heading.

Shell-smocked Hair Comb Ribbons:

- 6" (15 cm) satin ribbon, 1½" (39 mm) wide, for shell-smocked center
- 1 yd. (0.92 m) green satin ribbon, 1½" (39 mm) wide, for leaves

Other Materials:

- Hair comb, 3" (7.5 cm) wide
- Needle and thread
- FabriTac™ glue

Shell-smocked Hair Comb

1. Shell-smock (page 17) ribbon for the comb center. Fold ends wrong sides together and stitch diagonally to complete shell pattern; trim close to stitching.

2. Make six folded leaves (page 28), using 6" (15 cm) of green ribbon for each.

3. Glue the leaves in two rows to the heading of the comb, with gathered ends abutting in the center. Glue the shell-smocked piece over the top of the leaves, hiding the raw ends.

Headband Ribbons:

- Light green silk ribbon, for leaves and calyxes, 4 mm
- Lavender (or desired color) silk ribbon, for rose buds, 4 mm

Other Materials:

- Light green embroidery floss for vine
- Wilton's Satin and Pearl Headband
- Flexible plastic template material
- Small curved needle, usually found in needle assortment packs in the notions department
- Tapestry needle

Stitch Key
for Headband

	Whipped Running Stitch
	Padded Straight Stitch
	Straight Stitch
	Ribbon Stitch

Headband

Artist's Tip: *Markena discovered that a small curved needle is handy for working the stitches on this padded surface. Because you are unable to secure stitches on the back side of this project, begin each stitch or series of stitches by taking a tiny stitch that will later be covered by the ribbon. To end, bring the ribbon to the surface under a stitch, trim it short, and hide the tail under the stitch.*

1 Cut a strip of flexible plastic template material with one edge matching the vine shape. Use the template to mark the vine on the headband.

2 Using the small curved needle and two strands of embroidery floss, embroider the vine with the whipped running stitch (page 31); switch to a tapestry needle for whipping the stitches.

3 Mark the positions of the rosebuds. Stitch the rosebuds with a padded straight stitch, made by first stitching a short straight stitch and covering it with a slightly longer one. Trail the ribbon under the surface from one bud to the next.

4 Stitch a calyx for the first bud with two straight stitches that radiate from the same point at the bud base. Embroider a ribbon stitch (page 31) leaf just below the calyx of the bud, bringing the needle out of the fabric at the base of the next bud.

5 Repeat step 4 to stitch all of the calyxes and leaves, alternating the leaves from one side of the vine to the other.

Headband

Carole Rodgers

Carole Rodgers includes many talents among her services: designing, consulting, photography, teaching, and new product development. As an artist who enjoys ribbon embroidery and crafting ribbon flowers and ornaments, Carole has had numerous original designs published in magazines and books.

Flowers Sampler

An assortment of silk ribbon embroidery

stitches combine with cross-stitch

and backstitch in Carole's delightful ode to

flowers. The ready-made mat

and frame were carefully selected to

enhance the design, repeating the

deep burgundy details and complementing

the cool green words.

Flowers
leave part of their
fragrance
in the hands that
bestow them.

Ribbons:

- 5 yd. (4.6 m) rose silk ribbon, 4 mm
- 4 yd. (3.7 m) dark rose silk ribbon, 4 mm
- 3 yd. (2.75 m) burgundy silk ribbon, 4 mm
- 3 yd. (2.75 m) lavender silk ribbon, 4 mm
- 2 yd. (1.85 m) light yellow silk ribbon, 4 mm
- 2 yd. (1.85 m) yellow silk ribbon, 4 mm
- 2 yd. (1.85 m) bright green silk ribbon, 4 mm
- 5 yd (4.6 m) medium green silk ribbon, 4 mm
- 3 yd. (2.75 m) pink silk ribbon, 7 mm
- 4 yd. (3.7 m) turquoise silk ribbon, 7 mm

Other Materials:

- Medium green embroidery floss
- Dark green embroidery floss
- Cashel Linen, 28 count, off-white, 14" × 18" (35.5 × 46 cm)
- Picture frame, 11" × 14" (28 × 35.5 cm)
- Mat, 11" × 14" (28 × 35.5 cm), for 8" × 10" (20.5 × 25.5 cm) picture
- Mounting board
- Scroll frame or stretcher bars for 11" × 14" (28 × 35.5 cm)

Flowers leave part of their fragrance in the hands that bestow them.

Flowers Sampler

1 Stretch the fabric on a scroll frame or stretcher bars, keeping the grainlines straight. Mark the center with a pin. Stitch the lettering with two strands of medium green embroidery floss, using cross-stitches and backstitches.

2 Transfer silk ribbon design to fabric. Stitch leaves and stems, using 4 mm medium green ribbon, and following the stitch guide. Fill in lazy daisy stitches of leaves with bright green. Backstitch the stems for the cluster flowers, using dark green floss.

3 Stitch the turquoise flowers with ribbon stitches, using 7 mm ribbon. Stitch the lavender flowers with lazy daisy stitches.

4 Stitch French knots in the centers of the flowers, using light yellow for the turquoise flowers and brighter yellow for the lavender flowers. Stitch the green French knots at the tops of the two center buds.

5 Make the spider web rose, using the 4 mm rose ribbon for the spokes and wrap with the same ribbon to a diameter of ½" (1.3 cm); tie off. Change to 7 mm pink ribbon and continue weaving until the spokes are full; tie off.

6 Make lazy daisy stitches for the rose buds with 7 mm pink ribbon; fill them with 4 mm rose ribbon. Make the lavender bud with a lazy daisy stitch. Work ribbon stitches in green over the buds.

7 Make cluster flowers with French knots. Make three-wrap knots with rose close to the bottom of the stems. Make two-wrap knots with dark rose; make one-wrap knots with burgundy. Intersperse colors, keeping darker shades to the tip ends of the branches.

8 Mount and frame as desired.

Stitch Key

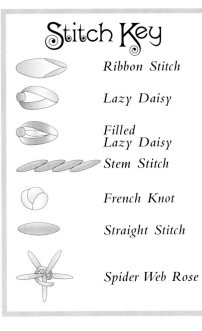

⬭	*Ribbon Stitch*
⬯	*Lazy Daisy*
⬯	*Filled Lazy Daisy*
〜	*Stem Stitch*
◯	*French Knot*
⬭	*Straight Stitch*
✳	*Spider Web Rose*

Ribbon Flower Shadow Box

by Janis Bullis

Four varieties of flowers were
borrowed from nature and made
entirely from ribbons to
be showcased in a dramatic shadow
box. Poppies, pansies, roses,
and strawflowers display a
variety of techniques and ribbon
styles in a colorful
arrangement. Janis selected black
velvet for the background
fabric in her shadow box, adding
depth and drama.

Ribbons:

- 3½ yd. (3.2 m) peach variegated wired ribbon, 1½" (38 mm)
- 1½ yd. (1.4 m) green wired satin ribbon, ½" (1.3 cm)
- 2 yd. (1.85 m) lavender variegated wired taffeta ribbon, 1" (25 mm)
- ¾ yd. (0.7 m) green variegated wired taffeta ribbon, 1½" (38 mm)
- 1½ yd. (1.4 m) sheer yellow ribbon, ⅞" (22 mm)
- ½ yd. (0.5 m) green double-faced satin ribbon, ¼" (6 mm)
- 2¼ yd. (2.1 m) feather-edged, double-faced satin ribbon, ¼" (6 mm)

Other Materials:

- Shadow box, about 10" (25.5 cm) square
- Black fabric backing, optional
- Needle and thread
- Hot glue gun
- Black embroidery floss, for poppies
- Five ½" (1.3 cm) black pompoms, for poppies
- Four ½" (1.3 cm) yellow pompoms, for pansies
- Eight gold-tipped stamens, for strawflowers
- Eight chenille flower stems, for strawflowers

Shadow Box

1 Make five poppies (page 19), using three 4-RW lengths of peach variegated ribbon for each. Crimp the dark edge of three outer layers; crimp light edge of inner layer. Tie a pompom in the center of six 3" (7.5 cm) strands of floss for each poppy center. Assemble poppies; set aside.

Artist's Tip: Observe the natural arrangements of petals on real flowers and pattern your ribbon flowers after them. But don't expect to duplicate every natural design. Instead, use some creativity and incorporate unusual materials or techniques that resemble Mother Nature's handiwork. Crimping the edge of the poppy petals is one example.

2 Cut three 10" (25.5 cm) pieces of wide green taffeta ribbon, for leaves. Fold in half crosswise. Gather along one long edge and across cut ends; pull up to desired fullness and knot. Set aside.

3 Make four pansies (page 27), using the lavender ribbon. Tie 4" (10 cm) piece of sheer yellow ribbon around a pompom for each pansy center. Insert ribbon tails through center hole and secure with stitches or glue.

4 Cut four 5" (12.7 cm) lengths of green satin ribbon for pansy leaves. Fold each in half crosswise; machine stitch at 45° angle from fold toward cut ends. Finger-press ribbon flat along stitching. Hand-gather cut ends. Set aside.

5 Cut seven 9" (23 cm) lengths of sheer yellow ribbon for roses. Gather each to about 4" (10 cm); knot. Roll into small roses, securing with stitches or glue. Attach small ribbon-loop leaves under each rose. Set aside.

6 Cut eight 10" (25.5 cm) lengths of feather-edged ribbon for strawflowers. Make strawflowers, using the open-end method (page 18) and taking ¼" (6 mm) stitches. Secure gold stamen to center of each; set aside.

7 Adhere black fabric to inner surfaces of shadow box, if desired. Lay out flowers and leaves on back surface, using the diagram as a guide. Secure the items, using hot glue; begin with leaves and strawflower stems, and layer flowers over the top. Assemble shadow box.

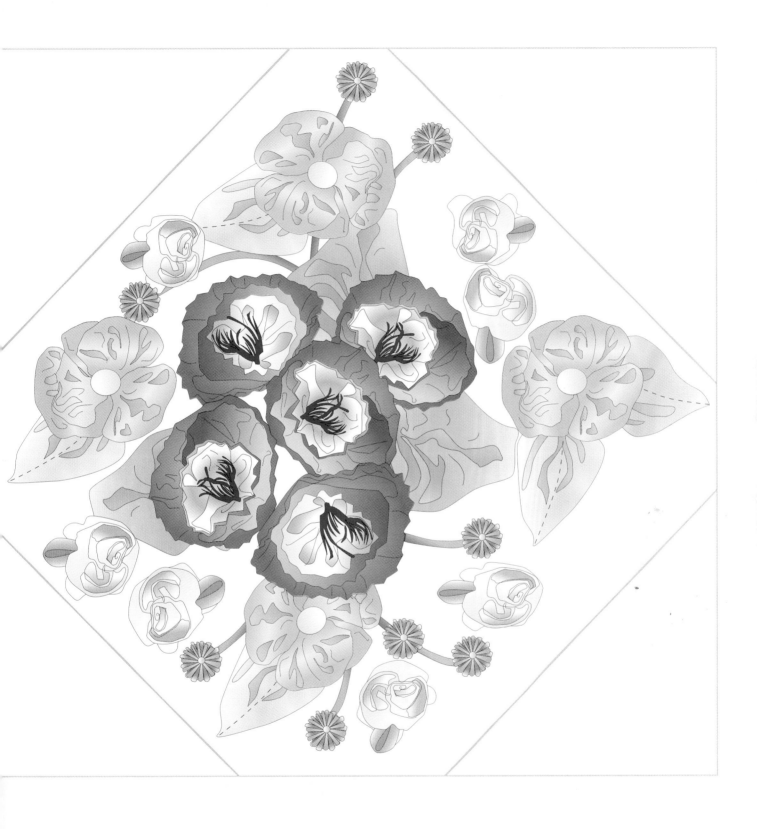

Ribbon Flower Wreath

by Carole Rodgers

Pansies and daffodils grace the curve

of a rustic grapevine wreath.

The unlikely combination of lustrous,

vibrant ribbons and rigid,

woodsy vine creates an artful contrast

of textures. Carole selected

flowers with colors that complement

each other, enlivening the

arrangement. Taking advantage of

the color gradations of ombré ribbon,

she created lifelike flowers

that even a passing hummingbird

could not resist.

Wreath

Ribbons:
- 2½ yd. (2.3 m) yellow ombré ribbon, 1½" (39 mm) wide
- ½ yd. (0.5 m) yellow ombré ribbon, 1" (25 mm) wide
- 1½ yd. (1.4 m) purple ombré ribbon, 1" (25 mm) wide
- 2 yd. (1.85 m) rose/cream ombré ribbon, 1" (25 mm) wide
- ¾ yd. (0.7 m) green ombré ribbon, 1½" (39 mm) wide
- 1½ yd. (1.4 m) green ombré ribbon, 1" (25 mm) wide

Other Materials:
- Mushroom hummingbird on a wire
- Grapevine wreath, 12" (30.5 cm) diameter
- Five round gold beads, 6 mm
- Five white stamen bunches
- 18-gauge stem wire
- Green floral tape
- Hot glue gun and glue sticks
- Scissors
- Needle and hand sewing threads in colors to match ribbons
- Straight pins
- Fray Check™

1 Make seven folded leaves (page 28), using 1½" (39 mm) green ribbon; set aside.

2 Cut two 10" (25.5 cm) pieces of the narrower green ribbon; make two calyx/leaf stems (page 28); set aside.

3 Make two pulled wire leaves (page 28), using 12" (30.5 cm) of the narrower green ribbon; set aside.

4 Make two large daffodils with wide yellow ribbon and one small daffodil with narrow yellow ribbon (page 27). Gather the darker sides of the ribbons toward the flower centers. Secure stamens with 5" (12.7 cm) lengths of stem wire.

5 Make one daffodil bud, using the wider ribbon: form two center cups, gathering the darker edges first. Cut 9" (23 cm) of stem wire; twist 1½" (3.8 cm) end around stamen bundle. Insert stem through center bud cup and base. Gather center bud cup tightly around stamens; gather base around center. Set aside.

6 Make a smaller daffodil bud, using only one layer of wide ribbon; gather ribbon with darker side on outer edge. Cut two 5" (12.7 cm) pieces of green ribbon for the bud calyxes. Gather the darker edge. Insert bud stems into centers of calyxes; wrap with floral tape. Set aside.

7 Make three rose/cream pansies and two purple pansies (page 27), using the 1" (25 mm) ombré ribbon. Stitch gold beads into pansy centers. Set aside.

8 Make one double-petal pansy section from each color for pansy buds, gathering lighter sides. Using the calyx/leaf pieces from step 2, glue the calyxes over the bud centers.

9 Lay out flowers and leaves on wreath, using the diagram as a guide. Secure the items, using hot glue; begin with leaves, and layer flowers over the top.

10 Trim the hummingbird wire so it can be hidden in the wreath. Glue the beak tip into a pansy center.

Artist's Tip: *Ribbon flowers and leaves secured to wire stems, especially those made with wire-edge ribbons, are very pliable. After securing all of the flowers and leaves to the wreath, bend the stems and arrange the petals into natural poses for a more realistic appearance.*

Janna Britton

As a fan of all kinds of ribbons, Janna's design experience includes projects that incorporate silk ribbon embroidery and cross-stitch on Aida cloth and needlepoint techniques on plastic canvas. She has woven satin ribbons for making picture frames, decorative boxes, placemats, table runners, and apparel accents. With a little imagination and know-how, Janna has turned grosgrain ribbons into Christmas trees and Santas and fashioned flocks of angels from satin and organza ribbons.

Woven Ribbon Photo Mat

Woven ribbons and fanciful flower embellishments on a purchased mat give a prized photograph special treatment. Janna selected various coordinating ribbons that draw out the colors of the photograph yet are subtle enough not to overpower it.

Ribbons:

- 1¼ yd. (1.15 m) light blue grosgrain ribbon, ½" (12 mm) wide
- 1¼ yd. (1.15 m) colonial blue satin ribbon, ⅛" (3 mm) wide
- 2¼ yd. (2.1 m) light green satin ribbon, ⅛" (3 mm) wide
- 1¼ yd. (1.15 m) light blue satin ribbon, ¼" (7 mm) wide
- 1¼ yd. (1.15 m) white iridescent ribbon, ⅜" (9 mm) wide
- 4½ yd. (4.15 m) white satin ribbon, ¼" (7 mm) wide
- 9" (23 cm) light green satin ribbon, ¼" (7 mm) wide

Other Materials:

- 8" × 10" (20.5 × 25.5 cm) white mat board with opening for 5" × 7" (12.7 × 18 cm) photo
- Picture frame with 8" × 10" (20.5 × 25.5 cm) opening
- Double-sided adhesive, 1½" (3.8 cm) wide, such as Peel n Stick™ by Thermoweb®
- Three 3 mm white pearls
- Three baby's breath flower beads, peach
- Thread, needle, scissors, ruler
- Low-temp glue gun and glue sticks
- Fray Check™

Woven Ribbon Photo Mat

1   Place mat face-down on work surface. Cut two 6" (15 cm) pieces of double-sided adhesive; adhere to centers of long sides. Cut two 4¼" (10.8 cm) pieces; adhere to centers of short sides. Keep paper backing intact.

2   Cut two 12" (30.5 cm) and two 10" (25.5 cm) pieces of each of the first five ribbons listed; cut four white satin ribbons in both lengths. Adhere ribbons to the sides in the order shown, with edges abutting, and ends extending beyond mat. Check for straight lines and complete coverage of the mat.

3   Cut four 1½" (3.8 cm) squares of double-sided adhesive; adhere one to each corner, keeping protective backing in place. Weave the ribbons for each corner one at a time; remove protective backing and adhere woven ribbons to corner.

4   Cut eight ½" × 1½" (1.3 × 3.8 cm) strips of double-sided adhesive; adhere to underside of mat at corners, keeping paper backing intact. Working one side at a time, remove paper backing and adhere ribbon ends to mat back.

5   Cut three 21½" (54.8 cm) pieces of white satin ribbon. Mark ¼" (6 mm) from each end; mark every 1½" (3.8 cm) between end marks.

6   Thread a hand needle with white thread; knot. Turn one ribbon end under, aligning first two marks. Pierce center of ribbon with needle going through second mark first. Alternating from one side of the ribbon to the other, continue piercing ribbon center at marks, forming loops that resemble ribbon candy.

7   Spread loops out evenly to form flower petals. Stitch back through layers to top of flower. Insert needle through baby's breath bead, pearl, back through baby's breath bead, and back through petal layers to underside of flower. Knot thread.

8   Repeat steps 6 and 7 for two remaining flowers. Using 9" (23 cm) of ⅛" (3 mm) green ribbon, form three loops and tack to underside of each flower.

9   Make three small flowers, using 3" (7.5 cm) of ¼" (7 mm) white ribbon in open-end method for gathering (page 18). Fold 3" (7.5 cm) piece of ¼" (7 mm) green ribbon into a figure eight and tack to the underside of each small flower.

10   Mark the locations of the flowers on the mat. Cut 14" (35.5 cm) of ⅛" (3 mm) green ribbon. Secure to mat at marks, using hot glue; drape ribbon gracefully between marks. Glue flowers to mat over ribbon at marked locations.

11   Insert mat into picture frame.

Artist's Tip: *If you prefer to use the woven ribbon photo mat without a frame, purchase a mat board that comes with a backing. Separate the two pieces before beginning the project. After decorating the mat, apply the backing and glue a cardboard easel or picture hanger to the back.*

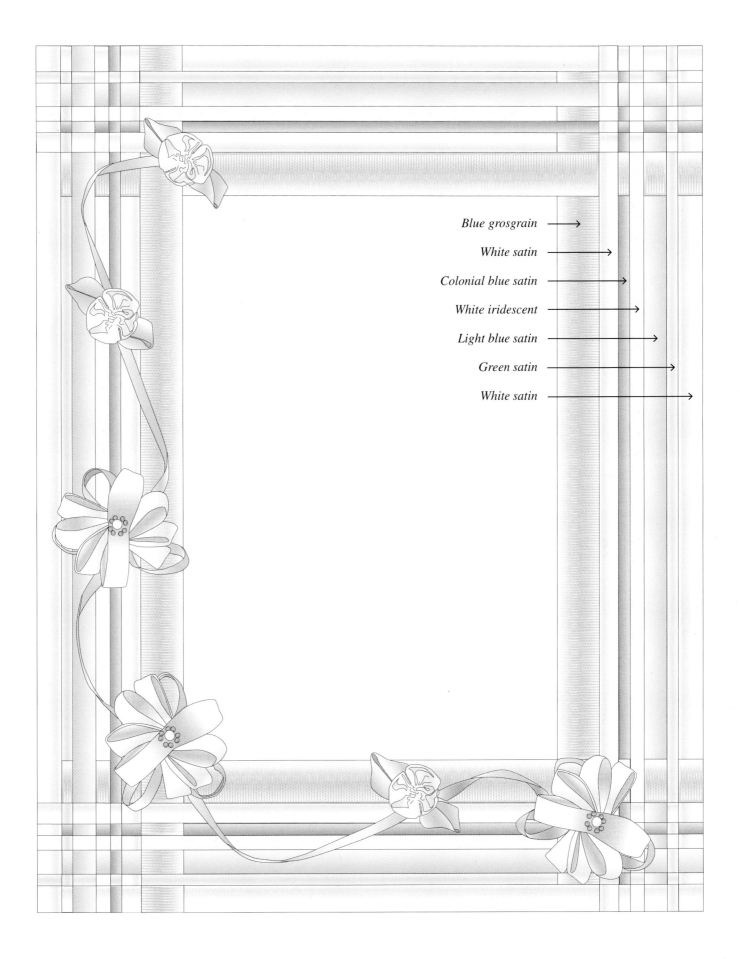

Blue grosgrain $\longrightarrow$

White satin $\longrightarrow$

Colonial blue satin $\longrightarrow$

White iridescent $\longrightarrow$

Light blue satin $\longrightarrow$

Green satin $\longrightarrow$

White satin $\longrightarrow$

Beverly Hofmann

Beverly Hofmann's designs for ribbon crafting are a combination of ribbon embroidery, needlepoint, cross-stitch, and bead work. She works the ribbons onto various materials, some of them rather unconventional, like perforated paper, Congress cloth, metal screen, mono canvas, and Aida cloth.

Ribbon Embroidery on Wire Mesh

Greeting cards that make lasting mementos are created by stitching silk ribbons onto copper, gold, or brass wire screen. The screen can be purchased in a roll or by the foot in plumbing departments of hardware stores or from a craft shop. The stitching method combines crewel, embroidery, and needlepoint techniques, using mostly straight stitches. Some of the designs are stitched by following a counted grid pattern. The wildflower designs are easier to stitch following a pattern printed to size on water-soluble stabilizer and basted to the screen. The finished designs are secured inside greeting card blanks that have cutout openings on the front. To obtain designs of the size needed to fit the cards, the screen should have a wire count of 14 to 16 per inch (2.5 cm).

Beverly creates floral design greeting cards that mimic the wildflowers native to the
Wyoming countryside where she lives. Her Christmas trees are accented with glass seed
beads, and the holly wreath sports a perky red silk bow. Handmade papers are used as backgrounds
behind some of the cards to add depth and texture.

All Card Materials:

- *Copper or bronze wire screen, 5" × 7" (12.7 × 18 cm)*
- *5" × 6½" (12.7 × 16.3 cm) greeting card with 3" × 5" (7.5 × 12.7 cm) rectangular or oval opening*
- *ModPodge® adhesive*
- *Handmade paper, 4" × 5½" (10 × 14 cm)*
- *Chenille needle, size 18 to 22*
- *Tapestry needle*
- *Masking tape*
- *Leather gloves*
- *Tin snips or heavy-duty craft scissors*
- *Water-soluble stabilizer for transferring floral patterns*

Basic Instructions

1 Cut a 5" × 7" (12.7 × 18 cm) wire screen rectangle, using tin snips or heavy-duty craft scissors; wear leather gloves to protect your hands from scratches. Apply masking tape around the outer edges to prevent snagging ribbons and scratching hands while stitching.

2 Transfer the floral designs to water-soluble stabilizer; baste to the screen front. Stitch the Christmas designs by counting wires in the mesh (page 91). Hand-tack ribbon tails to underside where they cannot be seen from the right side; trim short.

3 Remove stabilizer, if used. Remove masking tape; trim screen to 4½" × 6" (11.5 × 15 cm). Open card. Center design, face-down, over back of opening; secure with ModPodge glue. Secure handmade paper, if desired, to inside of backing flap. Fold backing flap over design, securing with glue on three open sides.

Wildflower Bouquet Ribbons:

- *Moss green silk ribbon, 4 mm*
- *Dark moss green silk ribbon, 4 mm*
- *Lilac silk ribbon, 4 mm*
- *Bright orange silk ribbon, 4 mm*
- *Yellow silk ribbon, 4 mm*
- *Bright blue silk ribbon, 4 mm*
- *Medium lavender silk ribbon, 2 mm*

Wildflower Bouquet

1 Stitch the flower stems with the stem stitch, using the two different colors of green silk ribbon.

2 Stitch the flowers with straight stitches. Stitch French knots in the centers of the daisy-type flowers.

Flower Trio

1 | Stitch the leaves with straight stitches, using the green ribbon.

2 | Stitch the flower petals with straight stitches, using the three colors of chiffon ribbon.

3 | Stitch French knots for the flower centers.

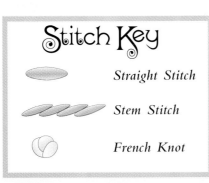

Stitch Key

Straight Stitch

Stem Stitch

French Knot

Artist's Tip: *To avoid bending the screen and to save wear and tear on the ribbons, insert the needle and pull the ribbon all the way through to the front or back with every stitch. While this takes a little longer than working stitches in and out in one step, the results are worth the effort.*

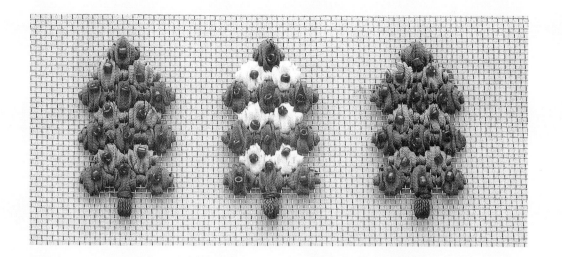

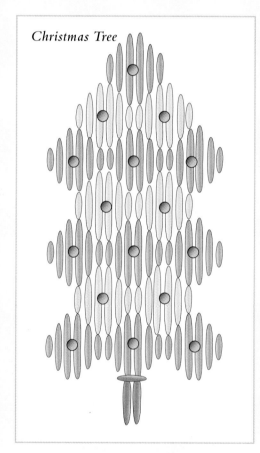

Christmas Tree

Christmas Tree Ribbons:

- *Moss green silk ribbon, 4 mm*
- *Dark moss green silk ribbon, 4 mm*
- *White silk ribbon, 4 mm*
- *Dark brown silk ribbon, 4 mm*

Other Materials:

- *Red glass seed beads*
- *Beading needle*
- *Fine red thread*

Christmas Trees

1 | Stitch the trees with straight stitches, using two shades of green for the outer trees and dark green and white for the center tree. Stitch the trunks with dark brown.

Artist's Tip: Don't be intimidated by the tiny squares. Think of the designs as clusters of diamonds. All the diamonds are exactly the same size. In adjoining diamonds, stitches from above and below share the same hole. Begin at the bottom and work the pattern in rows of diamonds.

2 | Stitch a red bead in the center of each diamond in each tree.

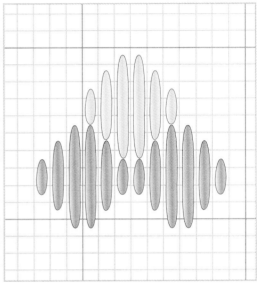

Artist's Tip: *Wire mesh may not be perfectly square; the wires may be slightly closer together in one direction than the other. For best results, work the patterns with the closer wires running horizontally.*

Holly Wreath Ribbons:

- *Moss green silk ribbon, 4 mm*
- *Dark moss green silk ribbon, 4 mm*
- *Dark red silk ribbon, 4 mm*
- *Red silk ribbon, 4 mm*

Holly Wreath

1 | Stitch the wreath with straight stitches, using two shades of green silk ribbon. Stitch double-wrap French knots where indicated for the holly berries.

2 | Thread 8" (20.5 cm) of red silk ribbon through two squares of the screen at the center bottom of the wreath. Tie a small bow; trim tails.

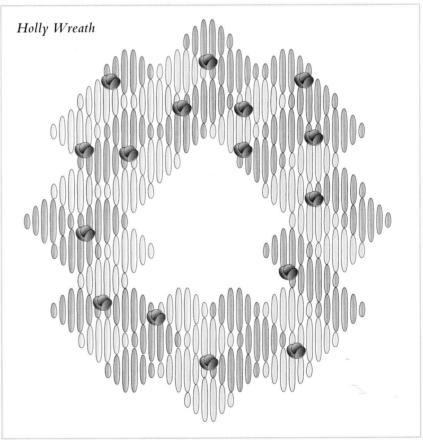

Holly Wreath

Grape Cluster Wine Bag & Napkin Ring

by Nancy Overton

Grape clusters, made by wrapping

wooden beads with ribbon,

are used to adorn the ribbon tie

on a quick-and-easy wine

bottle bag, cleverly fashioned from

sheer ribbons. The matching napkin

rings are a fitting complement

for any occasion, be it a romantic

Italian dinner for two or a

Saturday morning brunch. Another

grape cluster adorns the

brim of a summery straw hat. Wide

ribbon was lattice-smocked

to make a coordinating hatband.

Grape Clusters

Materials:

For grape cluster:
- *2 yd. (1.85 m) ribbon, 7/8" (23 mm) wide*
- *Eight 16 mm wooden beads with 3/8" (1 cm) holes*
- *24-gauge beading wire*
- *Tapestry needle with 1/2" (1.3 cm) eye*
- *Floral tape, 1/2" (1.3 cm) wide, brown or green*
- *Silk grape leaf picks*

For wine bag:
- *1 yd. (0.92 m) wired variegated ribbon for tie*
- *4 yd. (3.7 m) sheer wire-edge ribbon, 2" (5 cm) wide*
- *Materials for grape cluster*
- *Sewing needle and matching thread*

For napkin ring:
- *Materials for grape cluster*
- *Hot glue gun*

For straw hat:
- *2 yd. (1.85 m) ribbon, 3" (7.5 cm) wide*
- *Materials for grape cluster*

1 Thread tapestry needle with 8" (20.5 cm) length of 7/8" (23 mm) ribbon; run through bead, leaving 1 1/2" (3.8 cm) tail.

2 Wrap ribbon over bead and run through again. Repeat, slightly overlapping ribbon edges.

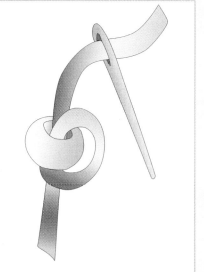

3 Wrap ribbon over bead to cover remaining space, bringing outside tail to inside tail; pinch tails together close to underside of bead.

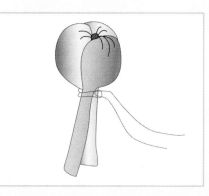

4 Wrap pinched ribbon tails twice with 8" (20.5 cm) length of beading wire. Twist remaining wire around ribbon tails. Wrap tail with floral tape, starting close to bead and covering entire ribbon and wires. Repeat steps 1 to 4 for all grapes.

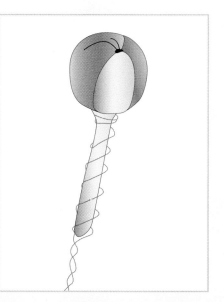

5 Arrange grapes in a pleasing bunch and wrap together with floral tape.

6 Cover a 10" (25.5 cm) piece of wire with floral tape. Wrap wire around pencil, leaving 2" (5 cm) straight, to make a curly tendril.

7 Add tendril and grape leaf pick to grape cluster. Wrap all together with floral tape.

Wine Bag

1 | Cut sheer ribbon into four 1 yd. (0.92 m) lengths; mark centers. Cross two ribbons at right angles, aligning centers. Cross remaining ribbons at right angles, and place over first set at 45° angles, aligning centers.

2 | Sew a running stitch around the center square created by the top two ribbons, catching all layers.

Napkin Ring

1 | Follow steps 1 to 6 for grape cluster. In step 4, wrap two of the grapes with 16" (40.5 cm) lengths of wire. Continue twisting wire ends together to end. Cut wire tail to 6" (15 cm) beyond cluster.

2 | Wrap cluster with floral tape, adding in leaf pick and tendril, and wrapping to end of twisted wire. Form wrapped wire into a 1½" (3.8 cm) circle just below cluster. Hot-glue end in place. Wrap connection with floral tape.

3 | Turn under ¼" (6 mm) twice on ribbon ends, encasing raw edges.

4 | Place wine bottle over center. Wrap ribbons up over bottle; tie with variegated ribbon, tying in grape cluster. Bend cluster to curve around bottle neck. Shape ribbon tails as desired.

Hat

1 | Measure the desired distance for the hatband. Multiply this length by 1⅓ to estimate the ribbon length needed for the lattice smocking section. Mark off and smock this length at the center of the ribbon, following the directions on page 17. Hand-tack band to hat front.

2 | Make a grape cluster, following steps 1 to 7. Hand-tack cluster to one side of hat over band.

Table Runner Set

by Janna Britton

Cheery and feminine, this table
runner dresses up a special breakfast
with its pretty ribbon flowers.
Napkin rings and a wicker basket
echo the theme with matching
flowers. It's like having a perpetual
vase full of garden flowers
to greet you every morning.

Table Runner Ribbons:

- 3½ yd. (3.2 m) moss green satin ribbon for edging, ⅝" (15 mm) wide
- 3 yd. (2.75 m) wire-edge purple ombré ribbon, 1½" (39 mm)
- 2 yd. (1.85 m) wire-edge fern green ombré ribbon, 1½" (39 mm)
- 2 yd. (1.85 m) wire-edge purple ombré ribbon, ⅞" (23 mm)
- 1 yd. (0.95 m) moss green grosgrain ribbon, ⅞" (23 mm)
- 2⅜ yd. (2.2 m) light blue wire-edge sheer ribbon, ⅞" (23 mm)
- 1⅓ yd. (1.27 m) lime green satin ribbon, ⅝" (15 mm)
- Ten light blue satin ribbon roses (ready-to-use)

Other Materials:

- 1 yd. (0.92 m) fabric, 44" (112 cm) wide
- 3½ yd. (3.2 m) fusible web, ⅜" (1 cm) wide
- Buttons in assorted colors and sizes for flower centers
- Thread in colors to match ribbons
- Sewing machine
- Iron

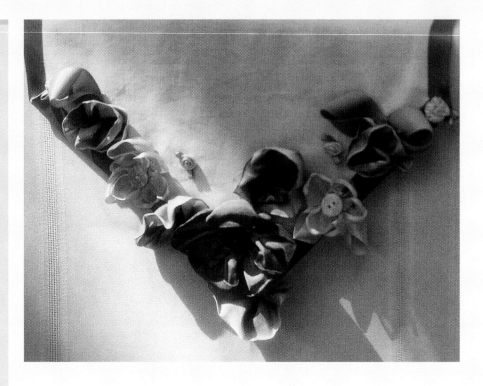

Table Runner

1. Cut table runner front 13" × 44" (33 × 112 cm). Mark center of short end; mark sides 6" (15 cm) from end. Draw diagonal lines from center to side marks; trim off fabric to make point. Cut opposite end to match; cut table runner back, using front as pattern.

2. Pin front to back, right sides together. Stitch ½" (1.3 cm) seam all around, leaving opening for turning on one long side. Trim seam allowances. Turn right side out, and press. Stitch opening closed.

3. Adhere paper-backed fusible web to wrong side of moss green ribbon, aligning one edge; follow manufacturer's directions. Remove paper backing, and fuse ribbon to table runner edge, allowing unfused edge to overhang runner edge slightly; miter ribbon at corners.

4. Make three five-petal flowers (page 20), using 24" (61 cm) of 1½" (39 mm) purple ribbon for each. Stitch buttons in centers. Set aside.

5. Make nine pulled wire leaves (page 28) for purple flowers, using 8" (20.5 cm) of 1½" (39 mm) fern green ribbon for each. Set aside.

6. Make seven light blue five-petal flowers (page 20), using 12" (30.5 cm) of ⅞" (23 mm) sheer ribbon for each. Stitch buttons in centers. Set aside.

7. Make six pairs of leaves for the light blue flowers, using 7" (18 cm) of wide lime green ribbon for each; fold ribbon into a figure eight and gather together at center. Make three folded leaves (page 28), using the same ribbon. Set aside.

8. Make six small purple flowers, using 12" (30.5 cm) of the ⅞" (23 mm) purple ombré ribbon for each. Pull wire on the dark edge to gather tightly; twist into loose spiral and hand-tack at base. Set aside.

9. Make three double leaves and one single leaf, using ⅞" (23 mm) grosgrain ribbon as in step 7 above. Set aside.

10. Arrange flowers and leaves on table runner ends, following the photograph above. Arrange remaining flowers and leaves in the table runner center. Hand-tack all items in place.

Basket Ribbons:

- *24" (61 cm) wire-edge purple ombré ribbon, 1½" (39 mm)*
- *27" (68.5 cm) wire-edge fern green ombré ribbon, 1½" (39 mm)*
- *12" (30.5 cm) light blue wire-edge sheer ribbon, ⅞" (23 mm)*
- *7" (18 cm) lime green satin ribbon, ⅝" (15 mm)*
- *24" (61 cm) wire-edge purple ombré ribbon, ⅞" (23 mm)*
- *Three light blue satin ribbon roses (ready-to-use)*

Other Materials:

- *Wicker basket*
- *Buttons for flower centers*
- *Low-temp glue gun and glue sticks*

Basket

1 | Make one large purple flower, one light blue flower, two small purple flowers, three large leaves, and two small leaves, following steps for table runner.

2 | Arrange items, along with purchased roses, on basket, following photograph. Secure, using hot glue.

Basket

Napkin Ring Ribbons

- *24" (61 cm) wire-edge purple ombré ribbon, 1½" (39 mm)*
- *22½" (57 cm) wire-edge fern green ombré ribbon, 1½" (39 mm)*
- *12" (30.5 cm) wire-edge purple ombré ribbon, ⅞" (23 mm)*

Napkin Ring

1 | Cut 4½" (11.5 cm) piece of 1½" (39 mm) fern green ombré ribbon; fold into thirds lengthwise. Overlap ends, forming a ring; tack securely.

2 | Make one large purple flower, one small purple flower, and two large fern green ombré leaves, following steps for table runner. Stitch leaves and flowers to ring.

Classic Silk Pillow

by Sandra McCooey

Like spindly asters reaching for the sun, tall,

slender flowers accent the sleek

styling of this unique pillow. To emphasize

the elongated design, the flowers are

stitched on the crosswise grain of a nubby

satin. The essence of simplicity,

the entire design is embroidered with only

one color of embroidery floss,

two colors of ribbon, and two embroidery

stitches. Ribbon tassels, made from

the same silk ribbons used in the design,

accent the four corners.

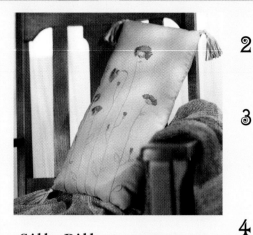

Silk Pillow

Ribbons:
- *Pale hunter green silk ribbon, 4 mm*
- *Copper silk ribbon, 4 mm*

Other Materials:
- *1/3 yd. (0.32 m) nubby-textured satin fabric*
- *Thread to match fabric*
- *Pale hunter green embroidery floss*
- *Sewing machine*
- *Polyester fiberfill*
- *Hand needle*

1 Cut pieces for the front and back of the pillow 11" × 20" (28 × 51 cm), with the length on the crosswise grain. Mark the design, running it vertically on the crosswise grain of the fabric, running the stems down into the pillow seam allowance.

2 Embroider the stems and leaves with the stem stitch, using embroidery floss.

3 Embroider the flower calyxes with the ribbon stitch, using the green ribbon. Embroider the petals with the ribbon stitch, using the copper ribbon.

4 Pin the pillow front and back, right sides together; stitch 1/2" (1.3 cm) seam on all four sides. Leave a 6" (15 cm) opening in the bottom seam.

5 Turn the pillow right side out. Stuff with fiberfill. Slipstitch the opening closed.

overlap line　　　　　*overlap line*

Stitch Key

Ribbon Stitch

Stem Stitch

overlap line

overlap line

Phyllis Dobbs

As a designer of ribbon embroidery patterns and ribbon manipulation crafts, Phyllis Dobbs has authored numerous booklets. Her original designs, which often feature vibrant colors, have been presented in many magazines and book publications.

Romantic Embroidered Pillow

This charming pillow features

a dimensional floral display that begs

to be touched and admired.

It is a lovely addition to a feminine

bedroom, with its

vivid colors and bold design.

Ribbons:

- 2 yd. (1.85 m) fuchsia/pink wire-edge ombré ribbon, ⅞" (23 mm)
- ½ yd. (0.5 m) fuchsia satin ribbon, ⅜" (9 mm)
- 1¼ yd. (1.15 m) light pink satin ribbon, ⅜" (9 mm)
- Periwinkle silk ribbon, 4 mm
- Medium pink silk ribbon, 4 mm
- Medium green silk ribbon, 4 mm
- Light green silk ribbon, 4 mm
- Light pink silk ribbon, 7 mm

Other Materials:

- ½ yd. (0.5 m) cream heavyweight moiré fabric
- 1⅓ yd. (1.23 m) cream satin twisted cording
- Clear glass seed beads
- Polyester fiberfill
- Thread: light pink, fuchsia, cream
- Sewing machine
- Hand needle

Romantic Pillow

1 | Cut pillow front and back 10½" × 14" (26.7 × 35.5 cm). Transfer pattern to pillow front piece.

2 | Fold 1 yd. (0.92 m) ombré ribbon into a bow with tails, following the pattern; hand-tack to pillow front, following pattern.

3 | Make a wired ribbon rose (page 24) with the remaining ombré ribbon, gathering along the lighter edge. Stitch the rose to the center of the bow.

4 | Make five light pink concertina roses (page 25) and three fuchsia concertina roses. Stitch to pillow front, following pattern. Stitch a clear glass seed bead in the center of each.

5 | Stitch the lazy daisy leaves, using two shades of green silk ribbon, following the pattern.

6 | Stitch the lazy daisy flower petals with medium pink silk ribbon. Stitch the loop stitch flowers with 7 mm light pink. Stitch colonial knots in the centers of the loop stitch flowers and in the cascading bunches, using the periwinkle ribbon.

7 | Pin the pillow front to the back, right sides together. Stitch ½" (1.3 cm) seam all around, leaving an opening for turning.

8 | Turn pillow right side out. Stuff with fiberfill. Whipstitch the cording over the seamline; tuck the ends into the opening, and stitch closed.

Stitch Key

- Lazy Daisy
- Colonial Knot
- Loop Stitch

Christmas Stocking

by Phyllis Dobbs

Imagine the delight in the receiver's
eyes when you present precious gifts hidden in
this even more precious Christmas
stocking. Ribbon-embroidered poinsettias
and roses cast against an elegant white
brocade background make this
stocking a Christmas memento that will
be treasured year after year.

Ribbons:
- Red silk ribbon, 4 mm
- Pale coral silk ribbon, 4 mm
- Coral silk ribbon, 4 mm
- Light gold silk ribbon, 4 mm
- Forest green silk ribbon, 4 mm
- Pale blue silk ribbon, 4 mm
- Medium green silk ribbon, 7 mm
- Green organdy ribbon, 5 mm

Other Materials:
- Pale blue embroidery floss or thread
- 1/3 yd. (0.32 m) white brocade fabric
- 1/3 yd. (0.32 m) white lining fabric
- Clear glass seed beads
- 8" (20.5 cm) white twisted cording
- Sewing machine
- Iron

Christmas Stocking

1 | Photocopy the pattern. Transfer outline of stocking to fabric; mark locations for flowers.

2 | Embroider the petals of the poinsettias with red and coral ribbon, using the stacked fly stitch.

3 | Embroider the leaves between the poinsettia petals with medium green ribbon, using lazy daisy stitches.

4 | Embroider the poinsettia centers with light gold ribbon, using colonial knots.

5 | Embroider the spider web roses, using pale blue ribbon and matching embroidery floss or thread. Embroider lazy daisy leaves with forest green.

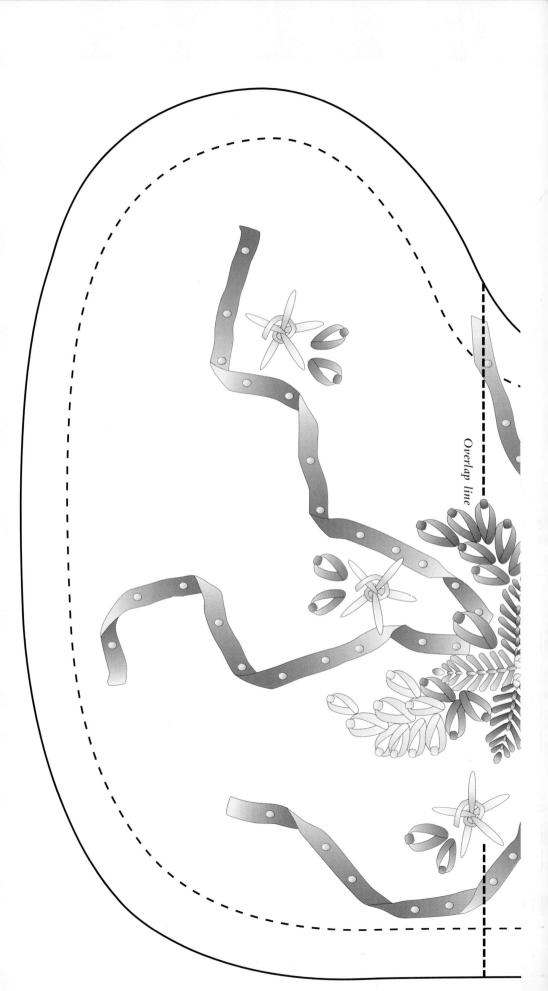

Overlap line

6 Embroider remaining petals with red and pale coral ribbon, using lazy daisy stitches.

7 Secure the trailing sheer green ribbon by bead couching.

8 Cut out the stocking front, allowing ½" (1.3 cm) seam allowance. Cut a reverse image piece for the back. Cut matching pieces for the lining. Pin stocking pieces, right sides together. Stitch, leaving top open. Repeat for lining.

9 Turn stocking right side out; slip inside lining. Pin stocking to lining, right sides together around upper edge. Fold cording in half; place between layers, aligning ends to upper edges at back seamline. Stitch ½" (1.3 cm) seam around top, leaving 3" (7.5 cm) opening on back for turning.

10 Turn stocking right side out; press. Edgestitch upper edge, closing opening and keeping lining from rolling out.

Stitch Key

Spider Web Rose

Colonial Knot

Lazy Daisy

Stacked Fly Stitch

Bead Couching

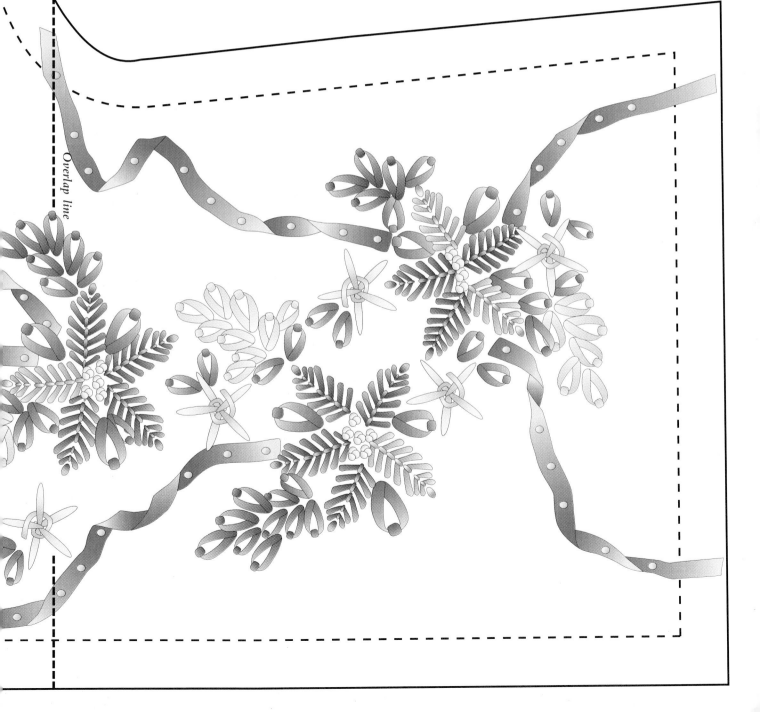

Overlap line

Index